CareerTransitions

Career Transitions provides immediate access to the most important career exploration and employment preparation activities. If you are college bound, on a vocational track, or preparing to enter the workforce, you will find an intuitive user experience designed to engage and guide you through practical learning activities and important education and career decisions.

Engaging, Interactive, and Focused

CT provides you with Personal Learning Experiences (PLEs) that are interactive and engaging. These include:

- Identify career inclinations through an engaging and eye-opening career interest assessment
- Browse through the Department of Education's 16 Career Clusters as well as spotlight career categories (including Green, New Economy, and High-Growth careers)
- Engage in a practice ride through real job situations with a customized, interactive interview simulation
- Create beginning resumes and cover letters with realistic samples and in-context tips and examples, and get practical guidance in the form of videos and short how-to articles
- Use a job and internship search to seek real opportunities for today and the future

Guiding Careers from Start to Finish

Career Transitions provides an intuitive user experience with direct access to a span of activities and information encompassing the entire career exploration and employment preparation arc.

SOUTH-WESTERN
CENGAGE Learning

FIRST-TIME REGISTRATION

1. Go to: **http://login.cengage.com/cb/**
2. Click **"Create My Account"**
3. Click **"Student"**
4. Enter your **ACCESS CODE** and click **"continue"**

> access code
>
> # PPFJSWWP53JQ3C
>
> duration: 1 year

5. Enter account information
6. Select your institution (school name)
7. Begin accessing **Career Transitions**

RETURNING USER

1. Go to: **http://login.cengage.com/cb/**
2. Enter your email address and password and click **"Sign In"**
3. Click **"Go"**
4. Click on **"Career Transitions"** to access

Enter your email and password in the spaces below and save this card for future reference. To access this resource you will ALWAYS need to return to **http://login.cengage.com/cb/** and enter your email address and password to sign in.

> Email

> Password

THE RESUME
WRITER'S WORKBOOK

THE RESUME WRITER'S WORKBOOK

MARKETING YOURSELF THROUGHOUT THE JOB SEARCH PROCESS

STANLEY KRANTMAN

SOUTH-WESTERN
CENGAGE Learning·

Australia • Brazil • Japan • Korea • Mexico • Singapore • Spain • United Kingdom • United States

SOUTH-WESTERN
CENGAGE Learning

The Resume Writer's Workbook: Marketing Yourself Throughout the Job Search Process, Fourth Edition
Stanley Krantman

Vice President of Editorial/Business:
Jack W. Calhoun

VP/Editor-in-Chief: Karen Schmohe

Acquisitions Editor: Michael Guendelsberger

Developmental Editor: Conor Allen

Editorial Assistant: Anne Kelly

Senior Marketing Communications Manager:
Jim Overly

Marketing Manager: Shanna Shelton

Marketing Coordinator: Julia Tucker

Internal Designer, Production Management,
and Composition: PreMediaGlobal

Media Editor: Lysa Kosins

Rights Acquisition Director: Audrey Pettengill

Rights Acquisition Specialist, Text and Image:
John Hill

Manufacturing Planner: Kevin Kluck

Senior Art Director: Tippy McIntosh

Cover Designer: Liz Harasymczuk

Cover Image(s): Main Image: ©Image Source/
Alamy; Left to right: ©Stockbyte, ©Patryce Bak,
©Chabruken, ©Tetra Images, Getty Images

For product information and technology assistance, contact us at
Cengage Learning Customer & Sales Support, 1-800-354-9706
For permission to use material from this text or product,
submit all requests online at **www.cengage.com/permissions**
Further permissions questions can be emailed to
permissionrequest@cengage.com

Library of Congress Control Number: 2011939333

ISBN-13: 978-0-538-49791-6

ISBN-10: 0-538-49791-2

Student Edition ISBN 13: 978-1-133-58924-2

Student Edition ISBN 10: 1-133-58924-3

South-Western
5191 Natorp Boulevard
Mason, OH 45040
USA

Cengage Learning products are represented in Canada by Nelson Education, Ltd.

For your course and learning solutions, visit **www.cengage.com**

Purchase any of our products at your local college store or at our preferred online store **www.cengagebrain.com**

Printed in the United States of America
2 3 4 5 6 7 15 14 13

CONTENTS

CHAPTER 4: CONTACT INFORMATION · 37

CHAPTER 5: CAREER OBJECTIVE · 47

CHAPTER 6: SUMMARY OF QUALIFICATIONS · 59

CHAPTER 7: PROFESSIONAL EXPERIENCE—CHRONOLOGICAL · 69

CHAPTER 8: PROFESSIONAL EXPERIENCE—FUNCTIONAL · 87

CHAPTER 9: EDUCATION • 111

CHAPTER 10: ADDITIONAL QUALIFICATIONS • 125

CHAPTER 11: REFERENCES • 133

CHAPTER 12: PUTTING IT ALL TOGETHER • 141

CHAPTER 13: THE COVER LETTER AND OTHER CORRESPONDENCE • 151

CHAPTER 14: THE JOB APPLICATION AND SKILL TESTS • 163

PART 3: THE INTERNET JOB SEARCH AND NETWORKING • 177

CHAPTER 15: THE INTERNET AND YOUR JOB SEARCH • 179

CHAPTER 16: ELECTRONIC RESUMES, PORTFOLIOS, AND OTHER NEW RESUME FORMATS • 193

CHAPTER 17: NETWORKING: UNCOVERING THE HIDDEN JOB MARKET · 207

PART 4: THE INTERVIEW AND FOLLOW UP · 217

CHAPTER 18: THE JOB INTERVIEW · 219

CHAPTER 19: PERSONAL JOB JOURNAL · 243

ACKNOWLEDGMENTS

I am sure most authors hope that once their book goes to print it is a finished product, thankfully never to be tampered with again. However, the area of job searching and resume writing is changing constantly, and much of what was the norm three years ago is no longer true. New approaches and tools are always being implemented. The advent of social media sites such as LinkedIn as well as a greater dependency on the Internet has changed many of our conceptions of job search. Detailed applications, in-depth interviews, and even psychological testing have become an integral part of the job search process. That's why a book of this nature is never "finished," and to actually meet the needs of the reader, it must be revised every few years to reflect changes and most recent trends.

Keeping this book up to date has always been a top priority to me, and to my publisher, Cengage Learning. I was enthusiastic when I was offered the opportunity to revise my book, and I am proud to say that this fourth edition you now hold in your hands contains the most up-to-date information on each topic covered. Also in this new edition, I have incorporated information and topics that both readers and reviewers have requested, making this edition more user friendly and comprehensive.

I am deeply indebted to the many people who made this book possible. My former clients at Capital Writers, whose resumes I prepared, truly provided me with the experience and background that formed the foundation of this work. Also, thanks to the many people I interviewed for this edition, who gave freely of their time and advice. In particular I would like to thank Christopher Townsend of Royal Banks of Missouri, Geoff Green of Brown Shoe, Inc, Stephanie Graff-Yaffee and Sharon Graff-Radell of TLC for Kids, and Pam Dixon of the World Privacy Forum.

My deepest appreciation to the excellent staff at Cengage Learning that painstakingly oversaw each phase of this revision, and whose attention to every detail resulted in a far better book than I would have produced on my own. In particular, I owe much thanks to Michael Guendelsberger, Acquisitions Editor, whose enthusiasm for this project is greatly appreciated. He has done an excellent job overseeing this project to fruition. I am very thankful that I was able to work with a developmental editor as talented as Conor Allen. Many of the improvements in this edition are a result of his keen insights, suggestions, and excellent editing work. He was always right on target and made my experience working on this edition more enjoyable.

To the excellent production staff, many whom I have not met personally but have seen their excellent work, I thank you. And last, but certainly not least, I would like to thank the many readers and reviewers—your advice has been invaluable and I thank all of you for your suggestions, many that I have incorporated into this edition.

Jeff Appel
Program Administrator, Design Department
Hickey College—St. Louis

Robin Delaney
Instructor
Hickey College—St. Louis

Joy Lawrence
Instructor
Heald College—Fresno

Donna Madison-Bell
Instructor
Heald College—San Francisco

Rita Springer
Instructor
Hickey College—St. Louis

Julie Stewart
Faculty
Hickey College—St. Louis

To all of you, my deepest appreciation. I couldn't have done it without you!

S.K.
St. Louis, 2011

PART 1

GETTING STARTED
CHOOSING YOUR CAREER GOALS

Overview

Before you embark on your job search and before you even think about your resume, it is imperative that you set a practical career objective. Keep your options open. Many job searchers, in particular students applying for first-time employment, have skills they're not even aware of. In an interview I had with Christopher Townsend, Assistant Vice President, Retail Sales Manager, Royal Banks of Missouri, he made this point clear:

> "Many times when I am at a restaurant for lunch, I marvel at how well the servers take care of their 'clients.' To succeed as a waiter they must have the same client service skills that are involved in my industry, banking. Before they even hit the floor, they have to remember close to a hundred menu items, while in my area of work, we are selling ten or less products, savings, checking, money markets, and so on. The skills they use in their capacity as waiters to please their clients are the same attributes they can bring to the table in a banking-finance relationship. To get to know someone and build a strong client report and to sell way less than a hundred items would seem a job they would be more than equipped for."

CHAPTER 1

INTRODUCTION

THE CHANGING ECONOMY AND JOB MARKET

In recent years the U.S. economy has undergone radical changes. Many companies are outsourcing work that traditionally been done in-house. Some are being forced to downsize due to decreased production of domestic goods. Computers and other high tech instruments are now replacing jobs that were once done by people. The result of all this is more layoffs and more people looking for jobs than ever before. In today's volatile market it is almost a certainty that you will change jobs at some point during your career. Being hired today doesn't ensure that you'll never have to conduct a job search again. Because so many jobs today are temporary, one must always keep abreast of the most effective methods of conducting a job search.

Keep up to date on the changing job market.

Monkey Business Images/Shutterstock.com

These changes have also affected the way you must conduct a job search. The fact that good jobs are more difficult to secure has resulted in a much more competitive job search market. To conduct a successful job search you must become adept and proficient in your methods.

While the resume and cover letter will always be a significant part of your job search, they are not enough. Employers are becoming alarmed about the prevalence of resume padding, and consequently, they are now relying more on detailed applications, background checks, psychological testing, and more intense interviews.

The rising cost of hiring and training precludes employers from taking chances on candidates that are either inadequately qualified or lack a strong desire to remain with a company. Additionally, the number of resumes that employers receive is mounting, forcing employers to use various supplementary means for selection. While a good resume is still essential, it is no longer the single foremost means employers use to screen applicants. Today's economy brings new rules to the game.

MAKING A GOOD IMPRESSION—ON PAPER AND ON THE INTERNET

While much has changed, the most important rule of your job search remains: Make a good first impression. In the past, the first impression an applicant made was with their resume. Today, the first thing a perspective employer will most likely do is Google your name. He will scour the Internet in general and social media sites in particular—sites such as Linkedin, Facebook, and Twitter—to find out more about you. On one hand, this can be put to great advantage. If you post your achievements, professional recommendations, informational blogs and informative articles in your field, your potential employer may be most impressed—even more so than from just reading your resume. On the other hand, if you post offensive material—such as silly photos or politically disagreeable statements—you may ruin any chance you have of getting a call back. Job search guru Richard Bolles cleverly states that this combination of all the materials that the employer gathers about you on the web could actually be considered the "twenty-first century new resume." This new resume is always available courtesy of Google and can supply the employer with more information than you may want him or her to know. Therefore it cannot be stressed too much: Never post anything on the Internet that is detrimental to your professional image. In Chapter 15 we will discuss at length how to use social media sites to your advantage and what precautions you must take for both personal and security reasons.

The impression you make is not limited to your resume, interview, and information you've made available online, though. It extends to *every single contact* you make with a future employer or mentors who are able to put you in contact with people looking to hire. Be sure all your correspondence has a professional look, proper letterhead, and correct spelling and grammar.

Phone etiquette is an extremely important area as well, and one that is frequently overlooked. Don't have your phone answer with a message that is cute or childish. If your resume directs employers' calls to your home number, be sure the answering message sounds professional. When you phone a potential employer, you may want to prepare a written script so that, in a state of nervousness, you won't leave out any integral bits of information. A script may also give you more confidence as well.

Even your choice of an e-mail address reveals your level of professionalism. Addresses such as "redhotmama" could result in an employer dropping you off his contact list.

In short, **always and in all ways present a professional image**. This is perhaps the golden rule of your job search and as much as everything else might change, this will always remain the same. Remember, while many resumes look the same and sound the same to a future employer, the image that you present is unique. Be sure that it stands out from the crowd and presents you in your best and most professional light.

MORE EMPHASIS ON JOB APPLICATIONS AND SKILLS TESTS

Another major change in today's market is the emphasis employers are placing on job applications and skills tests. No longer relegated to entry-level positions, job applications are required for many managerial and high-level positions. Today's job applications have become more complex and comprehensive, with questions ranging from job experience and skills to job performance—topics previously addressed in the interview itself.

Additionally, more employers are now adding psychometric or psychological tests to their pre-interview screening process. Aptitude testing, including problem-solving assessment, has become quite popular. To reflect these changes, you will find an entire chapter of this workbook devoted to filling out job applications properly and information on psychological and skills testing.

Interviewing has become more intricate and complex as well. Here, too, employers are taking a more aggressive approach. Interviews are no longer simply talking about yourself and the job at hand; an increasing number of employers are utilizing behavioral-based interview questions. Many candidates are even undergoing a series of mock work assignments to simulate the daily pressures they will face in the job.

CHANGING ROLE OF THE INTERNET IN TODAY'S MARKET

The role of the Internet in your job search is also changing—for both better and worse. Fortuitously, more companies are managing their own dedicated websites where applicants can apply directly for jobs. This has proven much more effective than the numerous generic job boards where hundreds of jobs and thousands of resumes reside. Going straight to the source has always been one of the main principles of looking for a job. However, even when posted to a company's own website, a resume can get lost in the shuffle. When an employer has no idea where a resume is coming from, or if he or she can even trust its contents, chances are slim that this posting will result in an interview. The best way to get a job is and always will be by recommendations made to the employer by people he or she trusts.

While the success rate of posting a resume on a company website may be low, it has proven to be even less successful when posted on generic job search sites such as Monster.com. Unfortunately, these generic job boards have not only become overwhelmed with thousands of resumes, many have proven to be a security threat. Today, applicants who post resumes on generic job boards may find themselves unknowingly victims of job scams and fraud, including identity theft. Important information regarding posting your resume safely on the Internet will be discussed at length in Chapter 15.

However, there are several areas in which the Internet can and will continue to play an important role in the job search:

1. **Gathering information about a company.** Not only will you find lists of job openings as they become available, but most sites will also supply you with detailed information about the company which can be crucial for the interview. Additionally, a company's own website can furnish information about the working conditions

and the job at hand to help the applicant decide whether the job truly interests him or her. This saves both the applicant and the company time.

2. **Using social media sites to network.** Networking was and will continue to be the key to getting a good job. Meeting people who can mentor you, help you, and recommend you to others will always be the most effective way to get your foot in the door. In the past you may have been limited to your geographical area for networking. With the advent of social media sites, the world is literally at your fingertips. You can meet and discuss issues with anyone, anywhere, and practically anytime on these websites. Some have taken an interest in helping others, while others just enjoy the camaraderie. In either case, you can "meet" people who will give you advice and, most importantly, put you in contact with people who are looking to hire someone with your credentials. It can put you directly into contact with potential employers themselves, who, if impressed, may call you in for an interview immediately. Not only can you build a network of other professionals, you can continue to stay in contact with people, such as past professors or coworkers, who can play an important role in your job search. You can also find friends and colleagues you may have lost contact with who are willing to lend a helping hand.

3. **Social media sites can be an excellent way to "build your profile" and display your abilities and work.** They provide a forum for you to post your resume, samples of your work, and recommendations from your peers or past employers. In short, you can create a strong positive impression on display for everyone to see. You might also maintain your own website where you can not only post your resume and work samples, but start a blog where you can discuss important issues that demonstrate your intelligence and expertise, guaranteed to make an impression on any future employer. Keep your blog posts career-related so as not to generate controversy and be sure they will put you in a positive light.

4. **Websites such as Yahoo.com can keep you organized.** In today's market, it's easy to become overwhelmed with the amount of paperwork that goes out—resumes, cover letters, and e-mails. There are also the multitude of phone numbers, names, and appointments that you must have readily available. While this workbook provides you with index pages in which to keep hard copies of this information, you should keep a digital version handy as well. Keeping an online address book and calendar will ensure you that your information will be safe and ready for use at all times; should your computer crash, your Yahoo.com calendar will still be safe and sound. Being organized is an essential key in your job search and you should make use of all available resources for convenience and safety's sake.

USING THIS WORKBOOK IN YOUR JOB SEARCH

Like the job market itself, this workbook has evolved to reflect the continually changing job search methods. It is an *up-to-date, complete,* and *comprehensive* job search manual designed to guide you through every step of the process. While many areas of job search may change, one thing always remains constant: Understanding how the job market works and mastering the various facets of job search (resumes, cover letters, networking, and interviewing) will give you the edge you need while looking for a job.

Remember, from the moment you send in your resume until the moment you are hired, you are being tested and compared. Every document, including your resume and application, will be scrutinized. Every interview question will be analyzed. You will be compared constantly to other applicants. Using this workbook and mastering the art of job search will help you earn the dream job you deserve.

WHAT THIS WORKBOOK WILL DO FOR YOU

The Resume Writer's Workbook is designed to give you the edge you need in today's fiercely competitive job market. The structure of this workbook will simplify the arduous task of conducting a successful job search. Written clearly and concisely, the material is presented logically so that you can master it quickly. In practical terms, this workbook will help you:

- produce a top-notch resume.
- write impressive cover letters.
- uncover solid job leads.
- use the Internet efficiently and *safely* in your job search.
- master and best use social media sites to your advantage.
- produce e-resumes and e-cover letters.
- complete job applications effectively.
- excel at interviewing.
- follow up after an interview.
- keep detailed records of all leads.
- stay organized during your job search.

THE JOB SEARCH PROCESS

The material is presented in short sections, and follows the logical sequence of the job search process. This workbook is divided into four parts:

PART ONE: GETTING STARTED—CHOOSING YOUR CAREER GOALS
- assessing your skills
- deciding on a career objective

PART TWO—THE RESUME & OTHER EMPLOYMENT DOCUMENTS
- assembling all personal data
- selecting the most relevant information
- describing your skills, experience, and accomplishments effectively using powerful action verbs while emphasizing employer benefits
- creating your resume with an eye-catching layout
- preparing an e-resume (an electronic or scannable version of your resume)
- personalized cover letter for each prospective employer
- applications, portfolios, and personal web pages and web postings

PART THREE—NETWORKING
- using the Internet to uncover leads and research potential employers
- networking and creating a profile on a social media website such as Linkedin

PART FOUR—INTERVIEWING

↝ researching a company and preparing for an interview

↝ learning what to expect during the interview

↝ following up after an interview

↝ keeping detailed records of all contacts

THIS WORKBOOK'S UNIQUE FORMAT

In the initial chapters you will assess your skills and career goals. You will learn the basics of conveying that information in an effective, high-powered resume. Based on your skills, work experience, and career objectives, you will choose the best resume format for your individual needs.

Next, each component of the resume will be presented in a single, easy-to-read chapter. You will compose your resume one section at a time, directly in the workbook on the worksheet pages. Experience has proven that concentrating on each resume section individually simplifies the process and keeps the writing structured and focused.

In order to better understand the process, let's look at a sample resume. On page 10 note the various headings of the resume. A resume is simply an outline. Like an outline it uses major headings to focus the reader's attention on one specific topic at a time. These headings are then followed by the facts and information that pertain to them. Note that the major headings in a resume include:

1. **Contact Information**—Includes your name, address, phone number(s), and e-mail address. (And, if applicable, a URL or Internet address to an online profile.)

2. **Objective**—Focuses the employer's attention on the specific job or job area you are interested in (and qualified to do).

3. **Summary of Qualifications** (optional)—Lists your most impressive accomplishments and skills.

4. **Employment History & Professional Experience**—The meat and potatoes of your resume. Here you can present your employment history chronologically—including your job titles, major responsibilities, skills, and accomplishments. Or you can present your major skills as subheadings followed by accomplishments and experience relevant to your career objective.

5. **Education**—Includes your degree, your school, and if recent, your date of graduation. If you are a graduating student with little or no experience this heading will precede your "Employment History" heading.

6. **Additional Information**—Lists computer skills, pertinent licenses, knowledge of foreign languages, continuing education, seminars, or anything else pertinent to your job that is important for an employer to know.

This workbook follows the order of these resume headings so that you can work on each one independently. Charts and worksheets are provided to help you assemble and organize your information. Instruction sheets at the end of each chapter explain how to select your most impressive information. After you have completed the worksheets, detach them. Chapter 12 describes how to organize and assemble the information. When you are ready to print your resume, the sample resumes at the end of the chapter will assist you in selecting an eye-catching layout.

In later chapters you will learn what must be done *after* you have created your resume, including individual chapters on:

↪ constructing an effective cover letter, as well as interview follow-up letters

↪ the job application form

↪ effectively using the Internet and social media websites such as Linkedin, Facebook, and Twitter

↪ converting your hard copy resume to an e-resume

↪ networking techniques—uncovering hidden job leads

↪ interviewing—with mock questions and answers

↪ staying organized—journal pages

In this edition a few new features have been added to make your job search easier and to increase your chances to succeed. At the beginning of each chapter you will find "Prepare to Succeed." Here you get an overview of the chapter geared to help you more easily assimilate the material that follows. "The Inside Scoop" provides tips from hiring managers and other experts who reveal their personal views on what works and what doesn't. A professional's opinion based on their experience will give you an extra edge. "Success Stories" will demonstrate scenarios that others have used successfully and will give you ideas on how to boost your resume and job search to higher levels. "Search and Research" will offer advice on using the Internet and other means of research to gain additional information and tips to augment the chapter's text. In those chapters that deal with organizing lists and data you will find a "Chapter Checklist" at the end of the chapter. Use the checklist to ensure that you have assembled all the proper information you need to fill out the worksheets and compose your job search documents.

This workbook and its features have been designed to help you succeed. Finding a job is a tough process, but if you follow this workbook diligently you will not only have a top notch resume and cover letter, but you will also master the vital job search skills that you need to succeed. Best of luck in all your endeavors!

Marsha G. Dubessy

999 Devil Drive
Satana Hills, IL 60099
(312) 666-9999
marshadubessy@aol.com

OBJECTIVE: DENTAL ASSISTANT

SUMMARY OF QUALIFICATIONS:

- More than 12 years of experience as Dental Assistant.
- Proficient in all areas of dental hygiene.
- Perform intra-oral procedures such as placing amalgam, polishing and removing dental cement, removing sutures, irrigation and taking impressions.
- Expertly construct models of teeth/mouth and polish models of plastic and plaster impressions.

PROFESSIONAL EXPERIENCE:

Sept. 2004 – Present   Dr. Roland Sanchez, DDS
Dental Assistant

- Assist dentist in **all procedures** including oral evacuations and mouth/tongue retractions.
- Chart all appropriate data of patients during exams and treatments.
- Develop and mount x-rays according to the type of procedure.
- Maintain daily schedules to ensure workflow efficiencies and patient flow.
- Oversee the cleaning, sterilization and maintenance of all equipment and instruments.

June 1999 – Aug. 2004   Dr. Jody Phelps, DDS
Dental Assistant

- Skillfully prepared restorative materials and dental cement.
- Expertly constructed models of teeth/mouth and polish models of plastic and plaster impressions.
- Sterilized instruments using autoclaves and chemical disinfectants to maintain accepted standards.

EDUCATION:

May 1999 – Completed degree in "Dental Assistant Training Program"
Maryville Mark College, Santana IL

OFFICE SKILLS:

Proficient in MS Word, Excel and PowerPoint

ASSESSING YOUR SKILLS & SETTING A GOAL

☑ Excellent
☐ Very good
☐ Good
☐ Average

Prepare to Succeed >>>

In this chapter you will be assessing your skills and deciding on a realistic career goal. Every component of your job search strategy, from your resume to networking to your interview, will depend on the goal or goals you set. Consider the following before assessing your skills and deciding on a job goal.

Think about the type of job you would like to have. Do you presently have the skills and talent to succeed at that job? If not, what would it take to acquire those skills? Do you have a backup plan—a temporary job you can take while you acquire the skills you need? Can you acquire the skills on the job or in an apprentice situation? Remember, setting a realistic goal means being able to handle the job in your present state—not three years from now.

If you cannot identify your skills on your own, there are many tests as well as job counselors who can help. Searching online can be helpful in locating a service or counselor that can assist you. In many cases, they can help you select a job goal that is realistic for your skill level or improvise a plan for you to retrain. Many government agencies as well as colleges and technical schools have such counseling services available.

SETTING A REALISTIC JOB SEARCH GOAL

Before you can begin a job search, you must decide on one simple goal: What job do you want? However, it must be a **realistic** job goal—a job that you not only want but one that you are already qualified to do. Being qualified does not only include having the education or skills to perform the job; it also includes having the emotional makeup or personality traits required. For example, you may be a skilled accountant, but if you have trouble concentrating for longs periods of time on numbers, you will find an accountant's job boring. You will not perform well enough to keep that job for any period of time.

Before deciding on a job goal, assess where your major interests lie. Some people are skilled in interacting with other people, while others are more suited to working with data, and yet others enjoy working with their hands. Balance your own preferences and do an honest evaluation of where you are most likely to succeed. Remember, technical skills can always be learned, but personality traits are hard to change. Decide which area you are best cut out for and design your goals accordingly.

SEARCH AND RESEARCH

One of the most comprehensive websites in helping you assess your skills and pick a realistic job goal is the United States Bureau of Labor Statistics: www.bls.gov. Here you will find articles on employment and the fastest-growing jobs. To find more information on these jobs, search online with the key words "fastest growing occupations."

In particular you will want to browse through the most up to date *Occupational Outlook Handbook:* www.bls.gov/oco. For hundreds of different types of jobs, the *Occupational Outlook Handbook* tells you:

- the training and education needed
- earnings
- expected job prospects
- what workers do on the job
- working conditions

In addition, the handbook gives you job search tips, links to information about the job market in each state, and more.

Another helpful website in helping you assess your skills sponsored by the U. S. Department of Labor, Employment and Training Administration is www.careeronestop.org.

To find other sites (as well as get in touch with professional counselors and testers), enter the following key words into a search engine: "skill assessment tools" or "skills assessment tests."

THE EVER-CHANGING JOB MARKET

Another important factor to keep in mind is which jobs are most readily available and most likely to hire. If your chosen job is not in demand, you will have little chance of being employed even if you have all the required skills. Many of yesterday's jobs no longer exist. People who were skilled in fixing a VCR will obviously find themselves without work today. Many job areas are becoming obsolete due to newer technological advances, so choosing a realistic career goal should also take into account which job areas are growing most quickly.

The U.S. Bureau of Labor Statistics' projections of the fastest growing jobs are updated every two years. Top careers are listed by those requiring bachelor's degrees as well as those that do not require a degree or require minimal training. Looking at such a list can be helpful on deciding on a career goal that will realistically yield high job returns. You may find you must go back to school to gain the skills you require, but it may be worth the investment if you seek a long-term job.

SKILL ASSESSMENT

YOUR ASSETS = YOUR SKILLS

Your value to an employer is directly proportional to the skills you offer. In the eyes of the employer, you are your skills. Remember, you are selling your combination of skills and talent to the employer. That is why it is crucial at the very outset—before you even decide on a career goal—to identify your skills, both technical and personal. It is your unique combination of skills and talent that you are advertising in your resume. Therefore, before beginning your resume, taking inventory of your skills and clearly knowing what you have to offer is crucial.

As mentioned above, skills are not always technical, nor only acquired through formal education. Inborn personality traits and self-management skills are also meaningful to an employer. Yet, most people tend to overlook these marketable traits when they prepare their resume.

Skills can also be acquired through experience—and not only employment experience. Often, volunteer duties can supply numerous skills for your inventory.

DECIDING ON A CAREER GOAL

The first question you must ask yourself is: What job do I want? Without a specific goal or job objective, writing an effective resume and conducting an effective job search is impossible.

Choose a realistic job objective—a job for which you are currently qualified. In choosing a realistic objective the following three choices are open to you:

The Same Job You Just Left

Most unemployed people prefer to seek the same job they held previously. They are familiar with the work and already have the skills and experience for the necessary tasks.

The *Occupational Outlook Handbook* (www.bls.gov/oco) will keep you up to date on the ever-changing job market.

A New Job—But One that Utilizes the Same General Skills

Some unemployed individuals opt for a change. The most logical job change would be one that uses the same skills in a different setting. In this situation you would have to prepare a resume that highlights your transferable skills (see discussion later in this chapter) and demonstrates to a future employer that you are capable of transferring your skills to new tasks and responsibilities.

A Career Change

If you want to change careers but do not have the skills or experience needed for the change, you can still implement a plan of action, such as one of the two below.

→ Return to school or begin an apprenticeship so that you can acquire the skills you need for your new career. This may require you to accept part-time work to make ends meet. However, if your goal is a new career, sacrificing in the present to build a more satisfying future may be worthwhile.

→ Opt for an entry-level position in the area you desire. For example, you may decide that you are suited to be a manager but that you have no experience. If you cannot return to school to learn management skills, you could apply for an entry-level position in sales and learn the ropes while you acquire the necessary skills to advance to management.

If you decide to take an entry-level position, be sure your resume demonstrates that you are equipped with at least the minimal skills required to *begin* a career in your desired field. Taking an entry-level position and learning on the job offers an opportunity for you to make a career change a reality.

If you are uncertain of what skills are required for a career change, *do some research*. Call people in the position you are seeking or call the personnel department and find out what skills are required for the job. If you can demonstrate in your resume that you have those skills, you'll have a better chance at landing the job.

TRANSFERABLE SKILLS

A transferable skill is simply a general skill used in one job situation that can be transferred to another job task without additional training.

THE INSIDE SCOOP

"We find that many college graduates who have earned their degree in early childhood development or even a degree in education may sometimes decide they don't want to work as teachers or administrators. Some may find it more satisfying to work as a nanny or in a daycare where they can put those same skills to use in a different environment."

Stephanie Yaffee, President & Sharon Radell, Agency Consultant,
TLC for Kids, St. Louis

For example, teachers use the skill of public speaking when addressing a class. That same skill can easily be transferred outside a classroom setting. Teachers could transfer this skill to a business setting and apply for a job training employees or conducting seminars.

If someone is proficient in a skill he or she enjoys, yet wants a change of jobs, then transferable skills should be stressed in the resume. Finding a job that fits his or her particular combination of skills would offer an excellent alternative.

TAKING INVENTORY OF YOUR SKILLS

The practice worksheet at the end of this chapter will help you take inventory of your skills. Taking inventory before writing your resume is crucial. Doing so will keep you organized and focused as you write, and it will also aid you in setting a realistic career goal.

To inventory your skills, use the lists that precede the practice worksheet. The following instructions will explain how to use these lists in completing the practice worksheet that follows.

You may want to create your own skill areas such as Transportation Skills, and list such tasks as truck driving, chauffeur, and so forth.

The idea is to list *all* of your marketable skills —general and specific.

If you cannot find three major skill areas in which you are proficient, look at the tasks listed under each skill area. If you have performed any such tasks, list them.

CAUTION: Many employers today are administering tests to verify applicants' skills. Be careful when listing skills (particularly technical skills) at which you are not proficient. Before listing these skills, ask yourself if you'd feel confident being tested on them.

Technical Skills

Most of these are job titles. Check any of the positions on this list that you have held. Be sure to include volunteer work as well. If you were involved in fundraising for an

THE INSIDE SCOOP

"Whenever I interview someone with a strong 'people skills' background, I tend to lean on hiring them even over someone who has some banking background. Although they may not see it as a strong transferable skill, I have found that nine times out of ten they tend to meet their sales quotas even better than the more traditional candidates because their sales skills and people skills are usually well honed and they can bring home the cross selling component that we need as a bank."

Christopher Townsend, Assistant Vice President,
Retail Sales Manager, Royal Banks of Missouri

organization, you may want to include skills such as bookkeeping, public relations, or sales and persuasion. Be thorough and list everything.

Next, prioritize these skills. First list your strongest skills—those most important for your job objective. On the practice worksheet, under the heading Technical Skills, rank your top four skills from this list.

Major Skill Areas

These are general skills used in numerous jobs. These skills are also transferable. Check the ones you are proficient at. Next, prioritize them, and choose three main skill areas that are the most important for the job you are seeking. Write them on the practice worksheet in the spaces entitled Major Skill Areas.

Specific Tasks

Under each major skill area, you will find a list of specific tasks. Check the tasks you have performed. Prioritize them. Then add them to your practice worksheet. Be sure the tasks you record correspond to one of the major skill areas you have listed.

Marketable Personality Traits

What are your most marketable personality traits and self-management skills? Most marketable means those that are most in demand for your job goal and are most impressive to your future employer.

If the job you are seeking is people oriented, be sure to emphasize people-oriented traits. Naturally, traits such as "loyalty," "dependability," and "works well under pressure" are qualities employers always seek.

Again, be selective and prioritize. If you are seeking a job as a manager, you may want to emphasize skills such as ability to motivate people, getting along with others, and being a team player. Conversely, accountants would emphasize task-oriented goals, because their job primarily deals with data, not people. They may want to stress such traits as being analytical, having an eye for detail, and working well under pressure.

CAUTION: Personality traits are subjective—not clearly black or white. Be sure you can support each trait with experience (professional or nonprofessional) or with recommendations from others.

Once again, select your three most marketable traits, and list them on your practice worksheet.

TECHNICAL SKILL AREAS

Account Management
Accounting
Administration
Administrative Assistant
Adult Care
Advertising
Appraising
Arc Welding
Architect
Artist–Illustrator
Assembly Line Work
Audio-Visual
Auditing
Automotive
Banking
Barber
Bookkeeping
Broker
Building Maintenance
Business Management
Buyer
Capital Development
Career Development
Carpenter
Cash-Flow Management
Cashier–Checkout
Chemistry
Child Care
Clergy
Clerk
Communications
Community Relations
Computer Sciences
Conservationist
Construction–Labor
Consulting
Consumer Affairs
Corporate Executive
Cost Analysis
Counseling
Curriculum Development
Customer Relations
Data Processing
Delivery
Department Manager
Designing
Development
Dietician
Drafting
Drama
Driving
Editor/Editing
Education
Electronics

Employee Relations
Engineering
Equipment Maintenance
Farm Work
Fashion/Clothing
Field Research
Filing
Film/Video
Finance
Fitness Consultant
Flight Attendant
Food Preparation
Food Services
Foreign Languages
Forklifting
Franchise Management
Gardening
Geology
Government Service
Graphic Design
Groundskeeping
Health Sciences
Hotel Management
Housekeeping
Import/Export
Insurance
Interior Design
International Business
Interviewing
Inventory Control
Jeweler
Journalism
Laboratory Technician
Legal Services
Loading/Unloading
Loans
Machine Operation
Mail Clerk
Make-up/Cosmetology
Management
Market Research
Marketing
Mathematician
Medical Services
Military
Modeling
Municipal Work
Music
Nurse
Office Management
Performing Arts
Pharmaceutical
Photographer
Physical Therapist

Physicist
Plumber
Police/Security
Printing
Product Development
Product Management
Proofreading
Psychologist
Public Relations
Publishing
Purchasing
Quality Control
Radio
Real Estate
Receptionist
Recruiting
Recycling
Remodeling
Repairing
Reporting
Research and Development
Retail Sales
Robotics
Sales Representative
Secretarial
Securities
Security Guard
Social Worker
Special Education
Speech Pathologist
Sports
Statistics
Supervisor
Switchboard
Systems Analysis
Teacher
Telecommunications
Therapy
Trade Shows
Training
Transportation
Travel Agent
Truck Driver
Veterinarian
Visual Arts
Volunteer Services
Waiter/Waitress
Warehouse Work
Waste Disposal
Word Processing
Writer
Other: _____
_____
_____

MAJOR SKILL AREAS: SPECIFIC TASKS

Management Skills

Administering
Analyzing performance
Coordinating programs
Delegating responsibility
Evaluating performance
Executing programs
Improving techniques
Increasing sales
Monitoring people and tasks
Motivating people
Organizing people and tasks
Planning
Prioritizing
Recruiting and hiring
Reorganizing
Restructuring
Reviewing
Scheduling
Supervising

Communication Skills

Addressing the public
Advising people
Arbitrating
Arranging functions
Coaching
Correspondence
Counseling
Directing people and tasks
Editing
Entertaining people
Fundraising
Handling complaints
Instructing
Lecturing
Meeting the public
Moderating
Negotiating
Persuading
Promoting events
Publicizing products
Public relations
Recruiting
Running meetings
Selling
Setting up demonstrations

Teaching
Translating
Writing press releases

Research Skills

Analyzing
Calculating
Clarifying
Compiling statistics
Evaluating programs
Indexing
Organizing programs and data
Summarizing
Systematizing

Financial Skills

Appraising
Auditing financial records
Balancing
Billing (A/P, A/R)
Bookkeeping
Budget management
Calculating
Computing
Forecasting trends
Invoicing
Payroll
Preparing taxes
Projecting future growth
Purchasing
Raising funds

Creative Skills

Conceptualizing
Creating new ideas and products
Designing
Developing new techniques
Establishing
Founding
Illustrating
Implementing
Integrating
Introducing
Inventing
Originating
Performing

Planning
Revitalizing

Clerical Skills

Arranging functions
Basic computer skills
Billing
Calculating
Cataloguing and filing
Compiling information
Coordinating itineraries
Correspondence
Dispatching
Editing reports/letters
Generating information
Monitoring
Organizing office
Prioritizing
Reading materials
Scheduling appointments
Systematizing information
Taking dictation
Typing
Writing reports

Computer Skills

Creating new software
Designing new systems
Entering data
Knowledge of programs:
   Accounting programs
   Database programs
   Languages (C, Java, etc.)
   Spreadsheet programs
   Word processing programs
Maintaining computers
Operating systems
Programming
Repairing systems

Other Skills

_____
_____
_____
_____
_____

MARKETABLE PERSONALITY TRAITS

Task-Oriented Skills

Accurate
Adaptable
Ambitious
Analytical
Artistic
Aware (i.e., of market trends)
Capable
Clear-thinking
Committed to growth
Competent
Conscientious
Creative
Dedicated
Dependable
Eager
Efficient
Energetic
Enterprising
Eye for detail
Farsighted
Flexible
Goal directed
Good judgment
Hardworking
High achiever
High energy
Highly motivated
Honest
Imaginative
Independent
Industrious
Innovative
Leadership ability
Loves a challenge
Loyal
Manages time efficiently
Methodical
Meticulous
Motivated
Optimistic
Orderly
Organized
Perfectionist
Persistent

Problem solver
Productive
Punctual
Quick learner
Realistic
Reliable
Resourceful
Risk taker
Self-motivated
Sensitive
Serious
Shrewd
Sincere
Team player
Thorough
Trustworthy
Verbal
Versatility
Visionary
Works well under pressure

People-Oriented Skills

Ability to motivate others
Communicative
Congenial
Cooperative
Courteous
Diplomatic
Eloquent
Friendly
Generous
Gets along well with others
Good listener
Helpful
Leadership qualities
Outgoing
Patience
Sense of humor
Sensible
Supportive
Sympathetic
Team worker
Tolerant
Understanding

CHAPTER 2 CHECKLIST

Look over your skill assessment list (page 21). For each skill you have listed, can you cite examples of when you've demonstrated that particular skill? Can you cite on-the-job accomplishments that support that skill? Do you have a license, a degree, or experience at a job that attests to your mastery of such a skill? On a personal level, do you have letters or recommendations from others that confirm your claims? A successful resume and job search must demonstrate to an employer that you've mastered the skills and talents the employer needs. If you can't support your claims, you will have a hard time getting a job.

On the website for the United States Department of Labor, you'll find the *Occupational Outlook Handbook* here: www.bls.gov/oco. Visit the site and search for a job you would like to have. What skills are listed as requirements for the job? Do you possess those skills? If not, consider revising your job goal to include only jobs for which you are qualified. Or, try to find out if the skills you lack can be learned on the job or with minimal retraining. In that case, be sure you can convince an employer you have the determination and drive to learn on the job and succeed.

CHAPTER 2 / WORKSHEET

SKILL INVENTORY PRACTICE

TECHNICAL SKILLS:

1. _____

2. _____

3. _____

4. _____

MAJOR SKILL AREAS:

1.

2.

3.

SPECIFIC SKILLS:

A. _____

B. _____

C. _____

A. _____

B. _____

C. _____

A. _____

B. _____

C. _____

PERSONALITY TRAITS:

1. _____

2. _____

3. _____

PART 2

THE RESUME AND OTHER EMPLOYMENT DOCUMENTS

Overview

Without doubt, the resume is *the* single most important job search document and everyone seeking employment must prepare one. In this section you will assemble a top-notch resume that will get noticed. However, today you need more than a resume. Cover letters, broadcast letters, and job applications are some of the other employment documents that are gaining more importance and this section covers those as well. In an interview with Stephanie Yaffee, and her sister, Sharon Radell, who operate TLC for Kids, a placement agency for babysitters, each stressed the emphasis they place on their web application form, a routine that is quickly becoming the norm with today's employers.

"Even though we ask applicants to attach their resume, we have found that most of the information that we need to know about them is not on their resume and thus the need for a detailed application form. How an applicant answers the questions on our form is crucial in our elimination process. We also check to see if applicants are articulate and if they have taken the time and effort to answer In complete sentences—presenting themselves as professionals."

THE IMPORTANCE OF THE RESUME

| ☑ Excellent |
| ☐ Very good |
| ☐ Good |
| ☐ Average |

Prepare to Succeed >>>

Now that you have assessed your skills and identified your career goal or goals, you are ready to lay the groundwork for your job search in general and your resume in particular. While other documents in today's job market, such as the cover letter and job application, have also come to the forefront, the resume remains the single most important job document in your job search. As such, you must carefully plan each section of your resume to produce maximum results. Competition today can be fierce and the number of resumes an employer will receive, particularly via e-mail, can be staggering. Yours must stand out. Also, in many instances, the resume has unfortunately, become the main method employers use to eliminate potential candidates whose resumes do not stand out.

In this chapter, you will learn how to translate your skills into *employer benefits*, one of the key ways you can make your resume stand out. After collecting and examining your entire work history and experience, you will learn how to select only the most pertinent and important information to include in your resume. When it comes to writing an effective resume, "less is more" is the key to success.

Next, you will be introduced to the main resume formats and will choose the one that is best suited for your particular job search goal. In some instances, where you may have more than one goal, you might need to tailor individual resumes targeted to each individual career objective. In this case, you may need to employ more than one resume format.

Finally, you will learn what must always be included in your resume and what must never be included in your resume, regardless of which format you use.

After mastering these basics, you will be ready to begin writing—with confidence that you can and will succeed!

WHY YOU NEED A RESUME

Before an employer will take valuable time to interview you, he or she wants to meet you—on paper. Impressing an employer with your resume can make all the difference.

The term *résumé* comes from the French and means *summary*. Your resume is exactly that: a summary of your qualifications, skills, and achievements. It shows a future employer what you have done. It details your skills, training, work experience, education, and most importantly, your accomplishments with past employers.

It should also inform the employer of your career objective (the job you are seeking) and communicate in a concise manner the benefits of hiring you. Having a superior resume—one that effectively displays to employers what you can do for them—is imperative. Matin Yate put it very concisely when he said, "If your resume works, you work; if it doesn't you don't!"

YOUR RESUME IS A "MARKETING TOOL"

You should think of your resume as an advertisement—one that advertises *you* to a future employer. You are selling your unique combination of skills, qualifications, experience, and personality. All of these qualities must be obvious from your resume. The best way to impress an employer is by creating a resume that reflects the *benefits* you have to offer, rather than merely enumerating a shopping list of skills. A resume that focuses on employer benefits, not just skills, will rise above the competition.

EMPLOYER BENEFITS VERSUS SUMMARY OF SKILLS

A resume should be results driven rather than skills driven. By reading your resume, the employer must *quickly* understand what advantages you offer his or her company. Think of yourself as a product and the employer as the consumer. How would you sell your product (yourself) to the employer?

When a leading soap manufacturer came up with a new formula for its detergent, it informed the public it had added a new ingredient, green crystals, and mentioned the scientific name. Ingredients and technical jargon mean little to the consumer. What sold the product was the manufacturer's claim that these crystals made clothes cleaner and brighter. Whether you are selling soap or your services, people want to know the bottom line: What can you do to improve their situation? What do you offer? In other words, why should they hire *you*?

Your list of skills may be impressive, but an employer is more interested in the specific benefits you offer. When you write your resume, highlight these employer benefits. For example, if you are proficient in desktop publishing, do not just list your skills or the computer programs you've mastered. Translate those skills into benefits. Tell the employer what you are able to do with your desktop publishing skills. Instead of stating, "proficient in Microsoft Publisher," state "ability to produce attractive brochures at a low cost."

Skills only indicate your *potential*, while benefits demonstrate your *actual accomplishments*—what you have achieved with your skills. An employer realizes that many applicants are well-versed in desktop publishing. Impressing the employer with what you have done and can do with your skills will propel you past the competition.

For another example, pretend you are proficient in spreadsheets. However, if you created a nifty phone/address book from a simple spreadsheet, this will certainly impress an employer. Many people can enter data on a spreadsheet, but demonstrating how you used this skill to accomplish a task efficiently will distinguish your resume.

For a student, a similar example may be cited. While many students will boast their degree, a high GPA, or high test scores, a practical accomplishment such as a unique project you were involved in or academic papers that were published or well received would certainly be considered "employer benefits" and important additions to your resume.

Determine which benefits are most important to your target employer, and then stress them in your resume. In order to do this, you must be in sync with the employer

TRANSLATE YOUR SKILLS INTO EMPLOYER BENEFITS

Look at the worksheet from Chapter 1. Try to take each of the skills you mentioned and translate them into a benefit or accomplishment. The more specific you are, the better. These are the benefits and accomplishments you will want to focus on and include in your resume. Even your personality traits can be translated into accomplishments. Your eye for detail may be responsible for emending spelling errors in important documents. Investigate each skill similarly to produce concrete benefits you can offer the employer.

SKILL: ACCOMPLISHMENT/BENEFIT:

1. _____
2. _____
3. _____
4. _____

PERSONALITY TRAIT: ACCOMPLISHMENT/BENEFIT:

1. _____
2. _____
3. _____
4. _____

and think like him. Ask yourself, "What do I offer the employer that should earn me an interview?" The answer should fall into one or more of the following categories:

→ my combination of impressive **skills**;

→ outstanding **achievements** (how those skills were used to produce results);

→ the **experience** required to do the job right (this can also include experience gained from volunteer work as well as school projects); and finally

→ outstanding **personality traits** (such as motivated, enthusiastic, etc.) including **solid work ethics** (reliable, honest, etc.).

If your resume reflects these basic characteristics that all employers seek, you will stand out above the competition. Remember, while many people have the same skills you do, few will translate those skills into benefits on their resume.

Benefits and accomplishments also help an employer visualize how you will perform on the job. The better an employer feels he or she can predict your performance, the greater your chances are of getting an interview.

THE PURPOSE OF THE RESUME IS TO GET YOU AN INTERVIEW

Many people erroneously think that a good resume will get them a job. There is not a single employer today who will hire anyone solely on what he or she has read in a resume. Employers want to meet you in person before they hire you. They want to substantiate the facts in your resume, they want to be convinced you have the right personality, and they want to be certain you will fit in with their work team. This requires

A resume only gets you an interview; the interview ultimately gets you the job.

an interview, or in some cases, a series of interviews. It's not the resume, but the interview that ultimately gets you the job.

However, it's the resume that gets you the interview! In today's market, many companies use resume-tracking programs that rely on a computer to select resumes, rather than a real person. Because the computer's selection is based solely on it's finding certain keywords in your resume, you must be meticulous in your choice of words and thorough in describing those employer benefits you offer. Today, you not only have to impress the employer, you have to impress his computer as well! The purpose of any resume, electronic or otherwise, is simply to get you an interview.

How often have you thought, "If only I had met with the employer in person, I could have convinced him that I was the right person for the job!" Your only chance is to compose an impressive resume, one that the employer will notice, so that you can meet the employer in person and get the job.

OTHER REASONS FOR A RESUME

Although the main purpose of the resume is to get you an interview, there are also other important reasons why one should prepare a resume.

→ To prepare yourself for the interview. Most employers will use your resume as a guideline when they interview you. They will ask you to explain in detail the

THE INSIDE SCOOP

"In my experience with hiring, I tend to throw out resumes which don't conform to standard formats. Artistic and "cutesy" resumes have no place in our industry (mortgage/law) or in any true business arena for that matter. I worry that the person who submits such a "free style" resume may be a nonconformist and to me that spells trouble. I personally look for resumes that conform to tried and true format and layout. It is what I expect from **all** prospective employees, whether it be for a secretarial position as well as a position in the business and law sectors of my company. Stick with the traditional and you can't go wrong."

M. Graff, President Graff Mortgage Law

statements you have made in your resume. Because of this, it is important that you steer clear on your resume of any subjects or work incidents that you do not wish to discuss during an interview. If a sales campaign or project did not succeed, do not mention that specific project in your resume.

↪ To organize yourself. Preparing a resume forces you to assess your skills. This in turn will help you evaluate the many employment options open to you. It will also help you plan an effective job search campaign.

↪ To let employers know that you are actively seeking employment.

↪ To give yourself a sense of security. Maintaining an updated resume is a good idea even when you're not looking for employment. You never know when you will want to seek a better job or just a change. Furthermore, in case you unexpectedly lose your job, having your resume updated and ready is wise.

↪ To have a calling card. It is there when you want to conduct informational interviews to test potential opportunities.

WRITING AN EFFECTIVE RESUME

Most positions generate hundreds of resume responses. Employers cannot read them all. Consequently, they will **quickly scan** the resumes. You sometimes have less than 15 seconds to make that all-important first impression. Therefore, your resume must be unique! Even in a situation where a computer is selecting the resumes, the hiring manager will eventually evaluate it. To ensure that your resume stands out in the crowd, concentrate on the three most essential factors in writing your resume:

Select Your Most Powerful and Impressive Information

Selectivity is the key to writing a strong resume. You have only one chance to make a first impression, so you must give it your best shot. Do not bore the reader with endless facts about your past employment. Being verbose and adding extraneous information (even if it is job related) will only detract from the important things you want to present—namely your achievements and benefits. That's why it is imperative that you select only the most impressive and *significant* information about your professional experience. Be concise.

If you are not sure which skills and benefits are the most important ones to highlight and select, check out similar jobs on the Internet. What are most employers seeking in a candidate applying for the job you've selected? If you can, talk to people who have similar jobs or who work for that particular company. Find out what problems come with the job. Find out the qualifications the employer is seeking. After you understand what the employer is looking for, construct your resume accordingly.

Write with Impact

Use action verbs to describe your accomplishments. Action verbs conjure up a positive image in the employer's mind and give you an advantage. Action verbs describe you as a person who accomplishes goals. They are also more concise and make your resume more readable. A detailed discussion of action verbs and how to use them appears in Chapters 7 and 8.

For electronic resumes, keywords count. These are usually buzzwords or catchphrases used to describe your job and level of proficiency. Chapter 16 will show you how to select powerful keywords.

Use an Eye-Catching Layout

The best resumes are one page long. If you have many years of employment experience, you may require two pages, especially if you are using a chronological format. However, under no circumstances should a resume be longer than two pages. The more concise it is, the better. Your most pertinent information should stand out with the use of all capital, boldface, or italic letters. You may also use bullets to draw the reader's attention to significant information.

Electronic resumes have their own unique layout to accommodate for ASCII text, which can be read and scanned universally by all computers. ASCII text can also be inserted into the body of any e-mail program, making it an advantageous option. We'll discuss ASCII-formatted resumes further in Chapter 16. In our highly technological world, it is essential to have both versions of your resume accessible at all times.

Before you can apply any resume layout, you must first choose the proper resume format best suited for your career goal. These formats are like templates—standardized

SEARCH AND RESEARCH

Having a unique resume layout—one that gets noticed and stands out—is crucial. However, protocol is also important and thus deviating too much from the norm could prove detrimental. Even within the limits dictated by protocol there is plenty of room to be creative, though. Unfortunately, many find it difficult to design a unique eye-catching format on a computer with a standard word processing program, especially those who are not artistically inclined. Instead of investing money in a resume service, consider looking online for free resume templates.

Many of the samples and templates you will find will work within a standard word processor, such as Microsoft Word. In fact, searching Microsoft's own site may be your best bet. Follow this link:

http://office.microsoft.com/en-us/templates/

Microsoft's page provides numerous resume templates and samples. Follow the directions on their web page to download these samples and open them in Word.

and traditionally accepted forms in which to present your pertinent resume information. Besides supplying an organized outline form which makes the resume easier to read and evaluate, these formats also act as excellent tools for prioritizing your information as well.

RESUME FORMATS

CHRONOLOGICAL VERSUS FUNCTIONAL FORMAT

To explain the two most widely acceptable resume formats used today, let's consider the example of Juan Ortega.

In 2009, Juan began working for Capital Corporation as a sales representative. His job was to sell software packages to high-profile clients like AT&T. In 2011, he began his own business as a computer consultant. His business failed and he is now looking for a job as a computer consultant for a large firm.

Below are two ways that Juan can present his employment history.

EXAMPLE: **CHRONOLOGICAL FORMAT**

2011 to Present
   CEO/President, Ortega & Associates
   • Designed and maintained hardware systems
   • Evaluated and implemented software

2009 to 2011
   Sales Representative, Capital Corporation
   • Designed program sales packages for large companies such as AT&T
   • Increased gross sales by 10 percent

EXAMPLE: **FUNCTIONAL FORMAT**

COMPUTER CONSULTING AND DESIGN
   • Designed and implemented hardware and software systems for large industries
   • Evaluated computer software

SALES AND SERVICE

   • Experienced sales representative, whose clients included AT&T and McDonald's
   • Developed marketing plan for Ortega & Associates, resulting in a 10% sales increase in 2010
   • Evaluated software packages for large corporations

2011 to Present   CEO, Ortega & Associates
2009 to 2011   Sales Representative, Capital Corporation

Look at the examples of Juan Ortega's work history. What are the main differences between the chronological format and the functional format? Both formats give Juan's background and experience. Both mention his skills and accomplishments.

The difference between them is emphasis; namely, what is accentuated and what is mentioned first.

The chronological format stresses:

→ dates and lengths of jobs

→ past employers

→ job titles

The functional resume stresses:

→ skill areas

→ qualifications

Glancing at the chronological resume, we see immediately that Juan was CEO of a corporation. This can be very impressive. Additionally, if Capital Corporation is a large, well-known firm, seeing Juan's relationship to that company would also be impressive. Initially, you may think that this makes the chronological format a good choice.

However, Juan has had two different jobs in a short time span. Looking at his experience from a time frame does not show a strong, steady work background. If he had worked for Capital Corporation for seven or eight years, then the chronological format, which would stress his ability to stick with a job, would be preferable. In reality, he held his present job for less than three years.

Therefore, his best choice is to emphasize his accomplishments, which are impressive. In this situation, the functional resume, which stresses Juan's skills and accomplishments, would be the better way to present his experience and background.

One advantage of the functional resume is that Juan can choose which of his skills to place first. If he were seeking another job in sales, he would place his sales skills first, even though his last job was not in sales. In the chronological resume, Juan would have to place his last job first regardless of his present career objective.

It is important to note, however, that even in the functional format Juan listed his dates of employment and the names of his past employers. Many who follow a strictly functional format will omit this information. Be warned: Your future employer will want to know whom you have worked for and how long you have worked for them. If it's missing, they may get suspicious and assume you are hiding something. Employers not only want evidence that you have the skills you claim, but they want to know where you got those skills and for whom you made your accomplishments.

With the functional format you still have an advantage. By mentioning your skills first and putting the emphasis on your skill areas, your employer will be favorably impressed before finishing your resume. When he or she finally reads your chronology, not holding one job for a long period is less likely to be an issue.

SELECTING THE RIGHT FORMAT FOR YOUR RESUME

To help you choose the format that best suits your needs, look at the two charts that follow. One lists the advantages of using the chronological format, while the other lists the advantages of the functional format.

Read the charts. Check the statements that apply to you. If you can see a pattern (most of your check marks fall in the same chart), then your choice of format is clear.

Some people have multiple job objectives and find that numerous statements in both charts are true for them. If you are pursuing a job in two diverse areas, you will need two different resumes.

For example, you may be thinking about a career change, and decide to apply for a job in a new but related field. Although you do not have any solid work experience in this new area, you do have the skills required for the job. Therefore, a functional resume that stresses your transferable skills would be the most appropriate. However,

Chronological Format

☐ I have held the same job for more than five years.

☐ My employment history is one of stability. I rarely change jobs.

☐ My past employer(s) is a prestigious company, well-known in my field.

☐ My job titles are impressive.

☐ I plan to continue in the same field as my past job.

☐ I have considerable experience but in one area only.

☐ I have a limited repertoire of skill areas.

Functional Format

☐ I am changing career fields.

☐ I have never held one job for a long time.

☐ I recently finished school and do not have any professional experience.

☐ I am reentering the job force after a considerable absence.

☐ I am proficient in many areas and have many skills.

☐ I have held many jobs in various unrelated work areas.

☐ Most of my work experience has been freelance or temporary.

☐ My skills fit in better with my present career objective than do my prior job titles.

like most people, you worry you may not get an interview due to your lack of experience. Therefore, to be safe, you also seek a job in your present career. For that, a chronological resume that stresses your present job title and your most recent accomplishments would serve you best. In this situation, two resumes are better than one.

SECTION HEADINGS

Before you begin writing your resume, having an overview of the standard, acceptable resume headings is important.

These headings are simple. Think of a resume as an outline of your total professional history. Like a standard outline, the resume is divided into outline headings or sections. These standard, general sections are found on all resumes and are guidelines in organizing your particular information.

These headings allow the employer to quickly scan a resume for pertinent information. Furthermore, because they have become standard protocol, employers expect to find them on your resume. Don't deviate from this format.

The following chart lists and defines these standard headings. Some of them, such as Summary of Qualifications, are optional. However, many optional sections are becoming common in resumes, and including them in your resume is usually best.

Resume Headings

CONTACT INFORMATION

Name, address, phone numbers, and e-mail address. You may also want to add your social media address such as "Facebook" or "Linkedin."
This informs employers how to reach you for an interview.

CAREER OBJECTIVE

It is the exact job title of the position sought.

SUMMARY OF QUALIFICATIONS

It contains short highlights of your most impressive qualifications for the job.
This can be anything from skill areas and accomplishments to personality traits.

PROFESSIONAL EXPERIENCE—CHRONOLOGICAL RESUME

This is a list of all past employment, starting with your most recent employer.
Give job titles and under each list a short description of your tasks and accomplishments for that job.

SKILL AREAS—FUNCTIONAL RESUME

Your general skill areas are section headings.
Under each skill area, list specific job tasks and accomplishments that demonstrate your proficiency in that skill area.

EDUCATION

Highlight your most recent degree, and the colleges or trade schools you attended.
List any awards, dean's lists, or school projects that pertain to your career objective.
If you do not have a college education, mention your high school and diploma.

ADDITIONAL PERSONAL INFORMATION

Mention only that personal information that pertains to your job objective.
For example: awards, professional associations, and publications.

HOW TO ORGANIZE THE HEADINGS

How do you organize the headings? As mentioned earlier, emphasis is the key. What would impress your future employer more, your work experience or your education?

If you are a recent graduate with limited professional experience, then your education would be more impressive, and you would want to emphasize it. Therefore, the *Education* heading would go before the *Experience* heading.

What if you have a strong work history but your most outstanding achievements are from jobs *previous* to your last one? What do you stress, your steady work history (chronological format), or your achievements (functional format)? You are worried that if you follow the chronological format, and list your last job first, your more impressive qualifications will be buried. In this case, you can use the more acceptable chronological format but include a short *Summary of Qualifications* to emphasize your most impressive accomplishments and skills first.

WHAT MUST *NEVER* GO IN A RESUME

Many employers examine resumes in hopes of finding flaws. Due to the large number of applications, employers may use the resume as a tool to eliminate prospective applicants—rather than one for choosing the right person for the job. Everyone understands that a resume that fails to depict the applicant as having the skills for the job will eliminate him or her from the competition.

However, people fail to realize that mentioning negative information (facts that bother the employer) can eliminate even the most highly qualified applicant.

How do you protect yourself? Be careful not to offer too much information. Keep your resume focused on your skills and accomplishments. Never mention personal information, controversial information, or anything negative about yourself. Never mention your race or religion. Marital status and political affiliations are also not pertinent to your job performance. Never mention salary requirements or reasons for leaving a prior job. Although these issues may come up in the interview, the resume is not the place for this information.

Never Mention

- race
- political affiliations
- religion
- salary requirements
- marital status
- reasons for leaving a past job

GETTING STARTED

The division of a resume into section headings makes it easier to write. The headings give you a system for organizing your information and allow you to focus on the most pertinent facts.

Once you have selected your format, chronological or functional, and the order of your section headings, you merely organize your particular information accordingly.

This workbook is designed to simplify your task. It is divided into the same sections as your resume.

It will guide you through each section of your resume, one at a time, and show you how to select the most important information in your unique background that applies to that section. It will also aid you in presenting your information with impact and using the right action verbs to express your talents best.

Remember, your resume must make an impact to attract attention. Follow this workbook, step by step, and you will have a resume that gets noticed.

Let us begin writing.

CHAPTER 3 CHECKLIST

Gather all your work records and records of employment history. Make a list of each employer, your job title, and the period you worked for them. If you are a student, make a list of any major project or course work that you excelled in that pertains to your job goal and would impress an employer. List *all* of your responsibilities on the job—tasks you excelled in, skills you have mastered, outstanding achievements, and particular improvements and revenue gains for which you were responsible. Which skills and tasks can be translated into concrete employer benefits? List them. Which personality traits would impress the employer? List as many as you can think of. You may also refer to the list of skills you worked on in Chapter 1 and integrate them into this list.

After you have finished your master list, analyze it. Eliminate information that does not pertain to your present job goal or that is not impressive. What you are left with will become the information you will want to include in your resume. Keep this list on hand as a reference as you write your resume, and as a guide to be sure nothing important is omitted from your final draft.

CONTACT INFORMATION

Name, (Job Title/Credentials), Address, Phone Number(s), E-Mail Address, Social Media Link, Web-Page Hyperlink

This is the information an employer needs in order to contact you for an interview.

Prepare to Succeed >>>

In this chapter, you will compose a letterhead that you will use on **all** your business and job search correspondence: your resume, cover letters, thank you letters, and follow up letters. Your letterhead must stand out, be professional looking, and include all of your pertinent contact information.

The letterhead may seem like the easiest part of your resume to assemble, but remember your contact information is **the most crucial information** on your resume. If you accidentally transpose numbers in your phone number, or letters in your e-mail address, potential employers won't be able to reach you! Even if your resume touts outstanding qualifications, no employer is going to take the time to look up your number if the contact information in your letterhead is incorrect. Check and double check!

Choosing an appealing format for your letterhead is also important. That not only includes the layout you choose but also the font, font color, font size, and effects such as italics and bolding. These all play a role in making your letterhead professional looking. Remember, the very first thing the employer will look at on your resume is your letterhead, so take the time to make it stand out.

Some stationary and copy shops sell stationary with fancy borders which if used properly can create a very unique letterhead that stands out and is professional looking. However, many of these preprinted borders are too artsy and busy looking and should be avoided. A simple, professional border, when used properly, can add to your professional look.

In this chapter, you will assemble all of your contact information and decide upon the layout and format to present it. The goal is to present a professional image right from the start.

HOW TO PRESENT YOUR CONTACT INFORMATION

Name

1. Use your full name—first and last. Do not add nicknames or titles, such as John Doe III, unless you use them professionally. The idea is to project a professional image, not a lax, overly friendly or a high-strung, overly formal one.

2. If you are *professionally* called by a nickname, such as Bob instead of Robert, you may want to include it in your contact information, such as *Robert (Bob) Jones*, or just simply *Bob Jones*, since this is how you want the employer to address you.

3. Make your name stand out. Use capital letters and/or boldface type. You may also consider using a larger font size for your name.

4. Disambiguate your name. If your name can be either masculine or feminine, such as Francis, you may want to add Mr. or Ms. in front of your name (Ms. Francis Smith), to spare your employer from a potentially awkward situation. You could also use a middle name if that would clarify your gender, such as *Terry Joseph Adams*.

Credentials, Job Title, Degree (Optional)

1. If you have an impressive degree or credential, you may want to add it to your contact information immediately following your name, such as *Jason Williams, M.D.*, or *Susan Strauss, PhD.*

2. If you are seeking a job similar to one you previously held, you may want to add your job title to your contact information as well, such as *Joel Green, Registered Nurse* or *Margaret Sullivan, CPA*. This immediately lets an employer know exactly who you are and what sort of job you are seeking.

3. You may want to have different versions of your resume. In applying for a job in your present field, you may want your credentials or job title displayed prominently in your contact information. If you are transferring to another job area, you will want to omit your present job title. For example, if you were a certified public accountant and now want to switch to sales, it will do little good to attach the job title of "CPA" to your name. In such a case it is better omitted.

Address

1. Use a permanent address. This gives the employer an impression of stability. Using a post office box gives the impression that you are a transient.

2. Do not use abbreviations, because they can be confusing. Spell out everything (such as *Street* instead of *St.*). The exception to this rule is the two-letter abbreviation for your state, which is the post office standard.

3. Put city, state, and zip code on one line. Be sure to put a comma between the city and state. Double-check your zip code.

Phone Number(s)

1. Use your area code—your resume could be sent out of town for review. Also, many cities today have more than one area code.

2. Leave a daytime phone number. This is important because most employers will want to contact you during business hours. At the least, you need to have reliable voicemail that you check regularly. If an employer calls and no one is there to receive the call, you may not get another chance.

3. In today's digital age, perhaps the best number to list is your cell phone number, especially if you are the only one who has access to it. Listing too many numbers on your resume can confuse an employer. If possible, limit your phone numbers to two: your cell phone and your home phone.

THE INSIDE SCOOP

PHONE ETIQUETTE IS IMPORTANT

"Believe it or not, I consider phone etiquette at the top of my list when deciding whether to interview a candidate. If he or she has a silly message on their answering machine, or if when speaking to him or her, I sense an unprofessional attitude or lack of enthusiasm, I don't call them in. Also, I feel it is bad manners and presumptuous for a candidate to call me by my first name without ever having met me. Although I wouldn't disqualify them because of that, I certainly make a note of it, and it may subconsciously influence how I judge them on the interview. Also, if I have a hard time getting in touch with someone by phone to set up an interview, if there are many other available candidates, the one who I can't reach may be eliminated at the get go."

Victor Siegel, President Investment and Insurance Consultants, Inc.

PHONE ETIQUETTE

Part of projecting a professional image means having proper phone etiquette. When an employer calls your home phone, he or she should not be greeted with a silly voice-mail message or one where your three-year-old announces that you are not home. And

Don't overlook the importance of proper phone etiquette.

Adrin Shamsudin/Shutterstock.com

in situations where a potential employer might hear your phone ringing, don't use inappropriate ring tones. Be professional at all times. If needed, get a dedicated phone line reserved for your job search.

E-Mail Address

1. In today's high-tech society, it is imperative to include your e-mail address in your contact information. Many employers actually prefer e-mail as a means to contact applicants for an interview.

2. Write your e-mail address in all lowercase and in a smaller point size than the rest of your contact information. See Example 1 for how this should look.

3. Double check your spelling; it is easy to transpose letters. Remember, one typo or even a misplaced period could result in losing the interview because the employer could not contact you.

4. Consider setting up a dedicated e-mail address devoted solely for your job search. This way you can keep your personal e-mails and job search correspondence separate. It will also aid you in organizing your job contacts. Never use your present work e-mail as your contact—especially if you do not want your boss or co-workers to know you are looking for a job elsewhere. If privacy is your main concern, use a dedicated e-mail address that no one else can access.

E-Mail Etiquette

As with your answering machine messages, projecting a professional image in e-mail communication is imperative. E-mail addresses such as "redhotmama14" or "hoosiersrus" do not impress an employer. Use a simple e-mail address, such as a combination of your first and last name or your last name followed by a number.

Website Hyperlink—Social Media URL

1. Consider including your website if you have a dedicated one. Many programs, such as Microsoft Word, will automatically create a web page hyperlink which will take the reader directly to your website or social media page. This means that if an employer downloads your e-resume, he or she only needs to click on the hyperlink to go to your website.

2. It's a good idea to post your resume as well as your professional profile on a professional social media network such as Linkedin. If you have done so, you will want to add the URL to your contact information as well. In many instances, directing the employer to these links may be more crucial to your getting an interview than the resume itself.

3. Make sure your website and profiles are appropriate for a wide audience. Many people prefer to furnish website information in a cover letter so that they can better control who accesses it. (See Example 5.) However, you may opt to have your website resume open to all and password protect only those pages to which you wish to give limited access. When you want an employer to view those pages, you can simply e-mail them the password. Later in the chapter on networking and social media we will discuss these issues at length.

EXAMPLES

The following are examples of ways to handle your contact information.

Study the different layouts and choose one that appeals to you. Any one of them would be a good choice for your resume and letterhead. As mentioned earlier, you can purchase stationary with preprinted borders, however, in most cases, a simple letterhead like the examples below are more than adequate.

EXAMPLE 1: MOST COMMON LAYOUT

This has become the most common layout, and you will not go wrong with it.

> **JUAN ORTEGA**
> 1124 Bakery Avenue
> Bakersville, NC 90000
> (555) 876-7876
> juano@sbcglobal.net

EXAMPLE 2: ANOTHER POPULAR LAYOUT

Arranging your name on the far right has a definite advantage. When an employer flips through a stack of resumes, yours will stand out. Thus, some experts prefer this layout.

> **JUAN ORTEGA**
> 1124 Bakery Avenue
> Bakersville, NC 90000
> (555) 876-7876
> juano@sbcglobal.net

EXAMPLE 3: A VARIATION OF THE PREVIOUS LAYOUT

This layout is pleasing to the eye only if all of your resume headings are left justified.

> **JUAN ORTEGA**
> 1124 Bakery Avenue
> Bakersville, NC 90000
> (555) 876-7876
> juano@sbcglobal.net

EXAMPLE 4: ANOTHER VARIATION

This is a nice layout if you want to put emphasis on your phone number. It is especially effective if you are listing more than one number.

JUAN ORTEGA

1124 Bakery Avenue
Bakersville, NC 90000
www.linkedin.com/juano12

Day Phone: (555) 876-7876
Home Phone: (555) 887-9087
juano@sbcglobal.net

EXAMPLE 5: A CONTEMPORARY LAYOUT

JUAN ORTEGA
1124 Bakery Avenue • Bakersville, NC 90000 • (555) 876-7876
website: http://umo.edu/juan12.html

EXAMPLE 6: ANOTHER VARIATION

This format highlights your name, and because it is so different, your resume immediately stands out from the others. It also makes for a professional-looking letterhead.

JUAN ORTEGA

1124 Bakery Avenue
Bakersville, NC 90000
(555) 876-7876
juano@sbcglobal.net

SEARCH AND RESEARCH

If you would like to see other sample letterheads, search online for "Letterhead" or "Letterhead templates." Microsoft Word and other word processing and desktop publishing programs have built-in capabilities to produce professional letterheads. There are also dedicated computer programs designed to create "stationary letterheads" as well. No matter which avenue you choose, keep it simple, yet professional.

C H A P T E R 4 / C H E C K L I S T

Before assembling your contact information, decide which phone number or numbers you are going to list. Do you have a proper and professional "answer message" set up on these lines? If not, do so now.

Have you set up a dedicated e-mail address for your job search? If not, you will want to do that now. In order to add this to your contact information, you must be sure it has been set up and is working. Test it by e-mailing yourself to be certain it is working.

Check your social media profile and personal website. Be sure nothing objectionable can be accessed by a potential employer. Remember the employer may Google you even before reading your resume and if something offends them, you will be eliminated immediately.

Look at different resume samples and even regular letterhead samples and decide on a format you feel projects a professional image that fits you. Decide on the font, the font size, and effects such as italics, bolding, capitalization. You may want to print out a few sample letterheads before deciding which one best suits you.

After you're finished, proofread your information. Be sure everything is correct. Be on the lookout for transposed numbers in your phone number information, and transposed letters in your e-mail address. When you are satisfied you will want to transfer this information to your worksheet.

WORKSHEET INSTRUCTIONS

On page 45, enter your contact information as you want it to appear on your resume. Study the examples on the preceding pages. Choose one. Arrange your information according to that layout.

Use a font that stands out, such as Bookman, Palatino, Arial, Century Schoolbook, Tahoma or any other serif font. (The serif fonts are easier to read than sans serif fonts, such as Helvetica.)

The Times Roman font has become the standard font used by most computer programs and as a result, most people today use it in their resumes and cover letters—and even in their letterheads. It has become so overused and common place that your best choice is a *different font*—one that will stand out, such as the various serif fonts mentioned above. A resume that stands out gets noticed and that is your goal. Choose a font that will stand out, yet one that is professional and not too avant-garde.

For effect, use bold or italic fonts, or even all caps. You may also change the point size of a font to highlight your name. For example, you may want your name in 16-point type and boldface, and the rest of the contact information in 12-point type. This way, your name stands out.

When you have finished, *proofread your information*! Be sure that your:

- ➔ address and zip code are correct.
- ➔ area code is listed with the phone number.
- ➔ day phone and home phone are both listed if needed.
- ➔ e-mail address is typed correctly.

CHAPTER 4 WORKSHEET

CONTACT INFORMATION

CONTACT INFORMATION:

_____

_____

_____

_____

_____

_____

CAREER OBJECTIVE

Specific job title of the position you are seeking

- This information indicates the job for which you are applying.

- It gives your resume a focal point, around which all the remaining information will be organized.

- An *effective objective* not only lists the prospective job title, but also informs employers of what you plan to do for them and/or the benefits you have to offer them.

| ☑ Excellent |
| ☐ Very good |
| ☐ Good |
| ☐ Average |

Prepare to Succeed >>>

In this chapter, you will learn about the importance of including an objective in your resume. If you plan to apply for more than one area of employment, it is best to prepare several versions of your resume each with a unique objective tailored for each job you are seeking. Sending out resumes designed specifically for each job objective can greatly enhance your chances of succeeding.

In this chapter, you will learn how to choose the right objective for your job search. You will see how you can use a job objective to mention important character traits that would otherwise not find their way into your resume. Most importantly, you will discover unique ways to beef up a job objective in order to distinguish yourself from the competition.

CAREER OBJECTIVE: IS IT REQUIRED OR OPTIONAL?

In past years it was common to find many resume experts disagreeing about whether a career objective should be included in a resume. Many experts felt it was best to omit an objective. They reasoned that if the objective was too specific, employers would not consider you for other jobs available outside of the one for which you applied, even if you were qualified. And if the objective was too general, it would appear as though you couldn't decide on a goal. Therefore, many felt that the place for stating your objective and career goals was in your cover letter.

Today, almost all experts agree that stating your career objective is a *Must*.

THE INSIDE SCOOP

Not every hiring manager feels the objective is important. "For me, the objective is important only if there is ambiguity in the resume. If I am looking at the resume of a person with diverse experience and I am wondering what does this person really want, that's when I go to the cover letter and the objective. Otherwise, the first thing I look at is their experience."

Geoff Green, VP of Talent Acquisition, Brown Shoe, Inc.

While many employers do not feel the objective is necessary, others want to see it. Without it, they may be uncertain where to place your resume and simply eliminate it from the start. This is especially true if you do a functional resume. Without an objective, a functional resume will lack focus and be confusing because you are listing your skill areas instead of your job titles. In that situation, it would be hard for the employer to know what job you are seeking; they might discard your resume altogether. Also, by not including it, you give the impression of being undecided about your career goals. Stating an objective shows that you know what you want. It demonstrates to the employer that you are goal oriented and serious about your career. In today's market, many employers will scan and file all incoming resumes. If there is no objective, personnel may be unsure of how to file your resume, and it will be discarded.

Furthermore, many companies have multiple positions open simultaneously. Without an objective, the employer may be unsure which position you are applying for and consequently not bother with your resume.

It sounds cruel, but put yourself in the employer's position. Most job openings generate hundreds of resumes. There isn't time to read them all. Thus, most employers initially scan them for keywords and pertinent information rather than reading them carefully. If they are intrigued, your resume will go into a pile for further consideration. If they do not find a catch word or a specific job title they are looking for, the employers will not consider your resume at all.

As you will discover in Chapter 15, many companies use computers to evaluate and select resumes. These resume-tracking systems search a resume not only for keywords, but also for objectives. Electronic resumes posted on Internet job boards and e-resumes sent via e-mail are almost always assessed by a computer. Most of them are catalogued by their objective—another reason why you must include one. That's why today, almost all experts agree that stating your career objective is a *must*.

Be sure the career objective you choose is *realistic*. Don't list an objective that you are not presently qualified for. Your objective should be the focus point of your resume and the rest of your resume should support your objective—demonstrating that you have the experience and skills to perform the job listed in your objective.

Beware of using too general an objective such as "seeking meaningful employment." Such an objective is useless. If you're submitting your resume you're obviously seeking employment! And every employer, without doubt, feels his employment is meaningful. Not only are such vague career objectives redundant, but they waste valuable space on your resume. Such a vague objective will not help an employer place

THE INSIDE SCOOP

"SEEKING ENTRY LEVEL POSIITON"—A BAD IDEA

"I don't think much of a resume which has 'seeking entry level position' as part of its objective. It sends the message 'I have no experience.' Even if it's true, don't broadcast that at the very beginning of your resume. After reading your resume, I will understand that you are a recent graduate with limited experience. I will understand that you are not seeking a top managerial position. However, I will understand all of that *after* I read your resume. This way, I will at least read your resume to the end. Don't put yourself at the bottom of the ladder from the beginning. Sometimes when I see 'entry level' I don't bother reading further. Don't take that chance with your resume. You may have just one shot and you could ruin it from the start.

'Seeking entry level position' makes you look desperate. To me it says, 'I'll take anything—just give me a job! Any job, even entry level!' No one wants to hire someone so desperate. Although every applicant is probably desperate to some degree, you don't need to give that away as a first impression."

—*Melvin Zuhler, President, American Eyewear Center*

your resume, nor will it be of any value to a computer generated evaluation. So when you write your objective, be *specific*. Focus on the exact job you are seeking.

While adding such a precise objective may limit your chances of getting *any* job, it will infinitely increase your chances of getting the job you want! In short, include your objective, but make it professional and effective!

HOW TO WRITE YOUR CAREER OBJECTIVE

Simple Objective

You can handle the objective on your resume in two ways. The simpler but less effective method is merely to list the job title you are seeking.

This approach is sufficient if you are using a chronological format and seeking the same job as your previous one—and if the entire emphasis of your resume is already on that job title and your accomplishments are in that area only.

EXAMPLE: **SIMPLE OBJECTIVE**

OBJECTIVE:	PHARMACIST

Use Your Objective as an Effective Marketing Tool!

Another reason to add an objective to your resume is that it can be a means of marketing your unique combination of skills—both technical and interpersonal. Your objective is the first thing the reviewer reads, and you can use it to make a great first impression. The secret is to focus attention on those skills that are most valuable for the job and to add *one* major benefit you can offer the employer. You should view your objective as a mini-resume, which summarizes why the employer should hire you.

An effective resume should be employer directed, as explained in Chapter 3. Its main purpose is to inform an employer of what you can and will do for their company. Displaying subjective skills in a resume can be tricky, since the major portion of a resume deals with previous employment, which does not lend itself to subjective analysis. One solution is to mention those skills in your objective. Here you may tell the employer something about yourself and your work ethic. You can add qualities

SEARCH AND RESEARCH

If you need help in formulating an exact job objective, a few pointers may be helpful. Take a look at the U.S. Department of Labor's *Occupational Outlook Handbook* at www.bls.gov/oco. Here you will find the most complete list of jobs and related jobs with their exact job titles and descriptions. Also, use the way a job is listed in the want ads as well as the job listings on company websites in your objective. In particular, when applying for a specific job listed, always use the precise job title in the listing as your career objective. Suppose a job post reads: Wanted: Member Service Representative. In your objective, rather than stating the general "Customer Service," you should use the exact phrase posted and state your objective as "Member Service Representative." Or if you are trying out for a secretarial position, rather than list "Secretary" as your objective, you may want to get more specific and list "Corporate Securities Secretary" or "Administrative Assistant" or whichever job title was used in the posting.

such as "my attention to detail," "ability to delegate," or any other *subjective* statement that puts you in a favorable light—right from the start of your resume.

You can also summarize the major contribution and benefit you will offer. For example, hiring you will result in "increased sales," or "a more efficiently run department."

In short, an effectively written objective allows you to make a *personal statement* in your resume. It gives you the chance to tell employers up front what you can do for them and what benefits they will gain by hiring you. Let us look at each step.

JOB TITLE

First, list the job title, as in a simple objective. Again, try to use the exact job title that appears in the job posting or the one stated in the Department of Labor's Occupational Handbook.

SKILLS YOU BRING TO THE JOB

Next, list your two or three top qualifications for the job. If you have many years of experience, you may want to list the number. If you have an outstanding accomplishment or unique combination of skills, you may mention that too. Adding one major personality trait that supports your objective is advantageous here.

EMPLOYER BENEFITS/RESULTS

Here you briefly state the employer's benefit in hiring you. That benefit can be increased sales, greater market shares, development of new products, or even increased efficiency. These are all benefits that every employer desires.

EXAMPLE: **EFFECTIVE OBJECTIVE**

> OBJECTIVE: PHARMACIST—where my nine years of experience, my expertise in generic medications, and my ability to fill orders quickly will result in increased efficiency.

WORKSHEET INSTRUCTIONS

Follow the instructions below to write your objective—one section at a time.

You will write:

- ↱ your job title.
- ↱ the skills and experience you bring to the job, including an outstanding personality trait important for your career.
- ↱ the main benefit you offer the employer.

When you have finished, you will compose your final version as you want it to appear on your resume at the end of this section.

WRITING AN EFFECTIVE OBJECTIVE

Use your Skill Inventory Worksheet (from Chapter 1) to assist you.

1. Job Title

Be specific. If you are seeking a job similar to one you have held in the past, that job title will be among those listed in your personal Skill Inventory Worksheet under Technical Skills.

If you are seeking a job in a new area, look at the list in Chapter 1 for examples of job titles. If the job you are seeking is from a job posting, tailor your job title to the one that appears in that post.

IF YOU ARE LOOKING FOR MULTIPLE JOBS IN DIVERSE AREAS, WRITE TWO RESUMES, EACH TAILORED SPECIFICALLY FOR EACH JOB.

2. Skills and Experience

What skills and experience can you bring to the position? Look at your list of skills from Chapter 1. Which of your general skills or, better yet, specific tasks will most impress the employer?

For example (a general skill and a specific task):

CUSTOMER SERVICE—where my communication skills and my ability to handle customer complaints will result in…

Or you may want to list your total years of experience:

CUSTOMER SERVICE—where I'll use my three years of experience in customer service to…

TWO IMPORTANT GUIDELINES:

1. MAKE SURE EACH TASK OR SKILL AREA THAT YOU MENTION IS RELEVANT TO YOUR OBJECTIVE. IN OTHER WORDS, IF YOU ARE SEEKING A JOB AS AN ACCOUNTANT, YOUR CARPENTRY SKILLS WILL NOT MATTER TO YOUR EMPLOYER. WHAT MATTERS WILL BE YOUR ABILITY TO AUDIT FINANCIAL RECORDS AND YOUR TOTAL YEARS OF ACCOUNTING EXPERIENCE.

2. MAKE SURE YOUR RESUME SUPPORTS THE SKILLS YOU MENTION IN YOUR OBJECTIVE.

Look at your Skill Inventory Worksheet. Choose your two most impressive qualifications that relate to your career objective. Alternatively, one skill area combined with one specific job task or your total years of experience in the field is also suitable. Choose two qualifications at maximum.

Have you omitted any skill areas from your list? If so, add them to your list in Chapter 1 now.

From your Inventory Skill Worksheet in Chapter 2, fill in any two of the blanks in Item 2 of the practice worksheet.

3. Personality Trait

Which one of your self-management skills would most impress an employer? Be sure it relates to your objective.

A personality trait is not something you must put into your objective. However, since this is the only place in your resume that you can make a subjective comment about yourself, the objective affords you the opportunity to make a statement such as "I work well under pressure," "I am a team player," and so forth.

You may want to check the list in Chapter 2 again for assistance.

4. Employer Benefits

What benefits can you offer an employer? On the practice worksheet is a chart of benefits that most employers look for. Look at the chart, and check the most important benefit you can offer. If the benefit you plan to bring to the job is not listed, write it yourself under the heading **Other**.

Make sure the benefit you check is one that you can realistically bring to the job and that the benefit follows logically from the skills you mention in your resume.

5. Putting It All Together

Use the following example as a guide to organize your information.

EXAMPLE: **OBJECTIVE**

OBJECTIVE: PERSONNEL MANAGEMENT—where my five years of management experience, my proven record in recruiting and training new workers, and my ability to motivate others will result in improved employee performance.

CHAPTER 5 / CHECKLIST

Before you write your Career Objective, decide what job you're seeking. Be sure the job title you have in mind is the same one used in the industry ads and websites. Pay attention to key words that are important for this job and see if you can incorporate any of them into your objective.

Are there other jobs that interest you? Make a list of all the possible career objectives you will need to compose. Will you have to stress other qualifications in these other objectives, or will you need do nothing more than just change the job title?

Decide how you will format your objective. You may want your job title to stand out in bold letters, or perhaps italics. Try a few styles and fonts to see which looks best to you. Remember, whatever style and font you choose will have to be used in the rest of your resume as well. Working on a computer, styles and fonts can all be reformatted once the entire resume is completed, so look at the formatting done now as a preliminary first draft which may change later.

CHAPTER 5 / WORKSHEET

CAREER OBJECTIVE PRACTICE

1. **JOB TITLE:** _____

2. **MAJOR SKILL AREAS IMPORTANT FOR THE JOB:**

    1. _____

    2. _____

    SPECIFIC TASKS / ACCOMPLISHMENTS NEEDED FOR THE JOB:

    1. _____

    2. _____

    NUMBER OF YEARS EXPERIENCE IN DESIRED FIELD: _____

    (Add this only if you have an impressive number.)

3. **MOST IMPORTANT PERSONALITY TRAIT NEEDED FOR THE JOB:**

    1. _____

4. **CHECK THE MAIN BENEFIT(S) YOU WILL BRING TO THE JOB:**

    ☐ Increase sales
    ☐ Improve system performance
    ☐ Increase market share
    ☐ Improve employee work performance
    ☐ Improve efficiency
    ☐ Promote good customer relations
    ☐ Develop new products
    ☐ Launch new products

    ☐ Create new programs
    ☐ Attract new clients
    ☐ Plan, organize and manage—budgets / departments / sales reps / etc.
    ☐ Improve staff recruitment
    ☐ Oversee and implement the newest technologies
    ☐ OTHER: _____

    (continued)

CHAPTER 5 / WORKSHEET (CONTINUED)

CAREER OBJECTIVE PRACTICE

5. **PUTTING IT ALL TOGETHER**

Transfer your information from the previous page to the chart below:

_____

(job title)

where my   _____

(skill #1 or years of experience)

_____

(skill #2)

_____

(personality trait—if applicable)

will result in _____

(benefit)

WORKSHEET INSTRUCTIONS

Compare the objective you wrote with the example at the bottom of page 53 and the previous example of the pharmacist on page 51.

Make whatever changes you need so that your objective flows smoothly.

Copy the final version of your objective on the worksheet page that follows.

Remember: Write it *exactly* as you want it to appear on your resume.

RESUME STYLE GUIDLINES

Your job title should stand out. To do this use either caps, italics, boldface, underlining, or a combination.

EVEN IF YOUR RESUME DOES NOT WARRANT A LENGTHY OBJECTIVE, DO NOT OMIT IT ALTOGETHER. AT THE VERY LEAST, LIST THE JOB TITLE OF THE POSITION YOU ARE SEEKING (LIKE THE EXAMPLE OF THE PHARMACIST).

REMEMBER: AN *EFFECTIVE OBJECTIVE*, ONE THAT MENTIONS SKILLS AND BENEFITS, WILL BE TAKEN THE MOST SERIOUSLY.

CHAPTER 5 WORKSHEET

CAREER OBJECTIVE:

CAREER OBJECTIVE:

SUMMARY OF QUALIFICATIONS

Short statements that highlight your most impressive qualifications and achievements.

- The purpose of the summary is to grab the employers' attention and impress them immediately. It should be customized to fit the job you are pursuing.

- To be effective, the statements must be concise, written with impact (action verbs), with an emphasis on keywords, and be results oriented.

- An effective summary will generate serious attention.

☑ Excellent
☐ Very good
☐ Good
☐ Average

Prepare to Succeed >>>

In this chapter you will prepare a "Summary of Qualifications" section for your resume. Some resume writers title this section "Professional Qualifications," some call it "Professional Profile" or "Career Highlights." A "Summary of Qualifications" is, in reality, just that—a summary; an encapsulated look at your most outstanding qualifications. This section is optional and an employer will not be disappointed if you omit it. However, when presented properly, this short summary can be a highly effective tool. By shining the spotlight on your most impressive achievements at the outset, you will grab the employer's attention immediately, resulting in reading your resume with heightened interest.

WHEN TO INCLUDE AND WHEN TO OMIT A SUMMARY

If you have a limited number of skills and achievements and you have already mentioned them in your objective, omitting the summary may be best. Mentioning the same skills repeatedly is overkill. Your resume will appear inflated, which may damage your chances.

On the other hand, if you are worried that an employer will overlook your impressive list of achievements if you bury them in the body of your resume, incorporating them in a summary is a good idea.

This rule applies particularly if you are using a chronological format, which focuses on job titles and dates of employment rather than skill areas. In such a case, highlighting your skill areas within the summary is wise.

Ljupco Smokovski/Shutterstock.com

Let employers know who you are and what you can do for them.

JEANETTE'S SUCCESS STORY—PUT YOUR BEST INFORMATION FORWARD

Jeannette M. was a top-notch educator. Besides having a PhD, which most of her peers lacked, she also single handedly developed a successful special education reading program that was already adopted by three of her area's schools. She also authored most of the reading materials used in the program. However, this accomplishment had taken place ten years earlier, two jobs ago. Although she mentioned this achievement in her resume, she was still having problems getting interviews for either "special ed teacher" or "special ed administrator."

Jeannette knew she had to rework her resume. Because she had a strong work history, she had chosen a chronological format to present her experience. Most applicants in her field used this format and most employers expected to see a resume in that format. The problem was that because her most impressive achievement was so long ago, she felt it was being buried in the later part of her resume and that many employers would not even bother reading that far. Her PhD degree was mentioned even further down in her resume under Education. She decided to make two simple changes to her resume which made all the difference.

First, she simply added the credentials "PhD" after her name in the contact information. Immediately on seeing her name, an employer would learn she held a PhD, a fact that alone made her stand out from much of the competition. Second, she added a Summary of Qualifications section at the beginning of her resume, mentioning her preeminent accomplishment first. Her most impressive information was no longer buried in her resume but highlighted at the very beginning. These simple changes helped her get interviews and in no time she snagged a position at a private school.

Let employers know immediately who you are. Arouse their interest and make them want to finish reading your resume. The better the impression you make, the better your chances for an interview.

Be sure to include keywords the employer will be looking for. Finding them at the forefront of your resume will also increase your chances of being selected.

A SUMMARY OF QUALIFICATIONS IS CRUCIAL IN TODAY'S MARKET

Besides prominently displaying your most important achievements up front where they belong, a summary can give you the opportunity to highlight many of the keywords an employer will be looking for. Seeing them as soon as possible may be instrumental in grabbing an employer's attention. In choosing the keywords for your summary, chose as many as you can that appeared in the job post. Also be sure to use those keywords and phrases that emphasize your achievements and employer benefits.

Another important benefit to using a summary is providing you a forum to present your transferable skills. With so many people changing jobs today, listing responsibilities used in prior jobs may not interest an employer who is hiring in another field. Someone who was a teacher and now wants to work in sales may find it hard convincing an employer they have the required skills. Reading their resume, the employer may see only what is obvious, the teaching skills that were used in past employment. However, in the summary, the applicant can translate those skills into transferable skills, demonstrating that they can perform in other arenas. Emphasizing transferable skills is especially important, not only for job changers, but for graduating students whose work experience is limited; these students can translate their classroom experience into transferable skills and place this information at the very start of their resume in their Summary of Qualifications.

THE INSIDE SCOOP

DEMONSTRATING A SUPERIOR WORK ETHIC MAKES A DIFFERENCE

"Sometimes when I look at resumes or interview potential employees it is very hard to distinguish between them. Many applicants list the same skills. Many of the recent graduates do not have a lot of experience and have all taken the same courses and acquired basically the same skills. It is becoming more and more difficult to decide which ones to call in for an interview and which ones to hire. One thing I have noticed of particular importance: I tend to lean towards candidates who convey a solid work ethic in their resume and especially during their interview. Honesty, loyalty, and dedication are important to me and are especially important for employees at a bank. I want to hire someone who enjoys working and believes in giving a job his or her all. If you can convey this in your resume you already have one foot in the door."

—*Christopher Townsend, Retail Sales Manager, Royal Banks of Missouri*

Remember that transferable skills are not only those you gleaned from past work. They can come from courses you have taken, or from projects you've taken part in at clubs or other affiliations. They can come from volunteer work, civic duties, and real-life situations. When emphasizing transferable skills, again, look for those skills that are most important for the job to which you're applying. A teacher may want to stress their ability to organize, train, and mentor among other skills needed in most areas of employment. A student may stress computer skills, problem-solving skills, research, accuracy, ability to work well in groups, and so on. The summary can be used to your advantage by allowing you to stress these skills at the beginning of your resume and focus on your strengths.

Another important aspect that you can focus on in your summary is your work ethic. It is not uncommon to find a summary that includes such statements as "team player," "hard worker," "loyal," "punctual," "cooperative," and "meets deadlines" among other subjective criteria. Sometimes it is these small additions that will make your resume stand out. One caveat, don't overdo the personality traits. One or two are enough. These are, in most part, subjective and will not carry a lot of weight. Listing too many of them will give the impression of padding and inflating your resume with hype.

HOW TO WRITE AN EFFECTIVE SUMMARY

SELECT THE MOST IMPRESSIVE INFORMATION

Your Summary of Qualifications is like a miniature resume. It focuses on the most important commodity you have to offer: your skills and accomplishments. Your summary is similar to an advertisement. As with an ad, each statement must be concise, full of punch, and impressive.

Which statements in an ad grab your attention? Those that solve a problem! Consider, as an example, these lines in an ad for a leading detergent: "Our detergent will cut your washing costs by 50 percent! Ours gets out even the most stubborn stains." Notice how these statements sell specific benefits.

You must do the same in your resume. You must sell yourself. Below is a list of ways to make your Summary of Qualifications sell you.

- ↱ List your most impressive qualifications—those that will be used to solve problems for your employer.
- ↱ List your most important accomplishments—problems that you have solved or results that you were directly responsible for in past jobs.
- ↱ List personal qualities that would impress an employer—those that will grab the employer's attention, such as "more than 15 years of experience," or "ability to work well under pressure." If possible, back these up with facts, such as "scored 97 percent on Managers' Training Test," or "was awarded 'employee punctuality certificate' for 2012".

WRITE WITH IMPACT

Going back to the detergent example, what do these statements have in common that catch our attention? They make claims that are results oriented. The ad tells us specifically how much we will save. The more detailed the statement, the more seriously we take it.

The same is true in your resume. Be specific. Do not make general statements such as "I saved the company money" or "I increased efficiency." Give details. Write

"I saved the company $4,000 in overhead," or "I increased efficiency by delegating more responsibility to staff members." The details add impact.

The second important principle is to write results-oriented statements. The previous examples give results: how much money you saved the company, and how you increased efficiency. Focus on problems you have solved for previous employers or proven results that you were responsible for achieving. Employers are interested in results.

CAUTION: Be careful not to overdo it. Limiting your summary to a maximum of six statements is best.

USE ACTION VERBS

Always use action verbs to describe your accomplishments. Chapters 7 and 8 discuss in detail the proper use of action verbs.

Because most of your summary's content will be a digest of your experience and accomplishments, you should write it last. First, complete the upcoming sections. However, before continuing, consider the following examples. They will give you an idea of an effective Summary of Qualifications. Return and write your Summary of Qualifications after you have finished the rest of your resume.

EXAMPLE: **A SUMMARY FOR A MANAGER**

SUMMARY OF QUALIFICATIONS	• Created successful questionnaire for evaluating work activities of personnel • Supervised turnover reduction of more than 60 percent • Received "Manager of the Year Award" 2009 • Ability to handle pressure and complete the job on time

WHAT ARE THE KEY ELEMENTS OF THIS SUMMARY?

↪ EACH STATEMENT IS CONCISE, DIRECT, AND RESULTS ORIENTED.

↪ ACTION VERBS (HIRED, TRAINED, CREATED, AND EVALUATED) ADD IMPACT.

↪ MENTIONING THE AWARD IN THE SUMMARY ENSURES THAT THE EMPLOYER WILL READ IT.

↪ ADDING THE PERSONAL QUALITY OF BEING ABLE TO HANDLE PRESSURE, A SITUATION EVERY MANAGER MUST FACE.

EXAMPLE: **A SUMMARY FOR A SECRETARY**

SUMMARY OF QUALIFICATIONS	• More than 10 years experience • Proficient in Microsoft Office • Evaluated office supply vendors for best price and reduced purchasing costs by 10 percent • Knowledge of light bookkeeping and payroll • Highly motivated team player

WHAT IS AN EMPLOYER LOOKING FOR IN A SECRETARY?

↪ EXPERIENCE—IF A PERSON HAS WORKED FIVE OR TEN YEARS AS A SECRETARY, HE OR SHE KNOWS HOW TO TYPE, TRANSCRIBE DICTATION, AND FILE. HERE EXPERIENCE IS A DEFINITE EDGE OVER THE COMPETITION.

↪ FAMILIARITY WITH WORD PROCESSING PROGRAMS—IN PARTICULAR, MICROSOFT WORD, THE LEADING WORD PROCESSING PROGRAM.

↪ BOOKKEEPING AND PAYROLL SKILLS—MANY SECRETARIES LACK THESE ABILITIES. MENTIONING THEM GIVES YOU AN ADVANTAGE.

When done effectively, the summary will give employers a positive image of you. It will impress them and entice them to read more. Be sure that the body of your resume supports and enhances what you have written in your Objective and Summary of Qualifications.

CAUTION: Although the Summary of Qualifications is one of the first sections appearing on your resume, you will write it last. It is a summary of your resume, and therefore, you should write it after you have finished your resume—when you can select your most impressive qualifications from the body of your resume.

Do not complete the following worksheet until you have finished the following chapters:

↪ Chapters 7 and 8, Professional Experience

↪ Chapter 9, Education

↪ Chapter 10, Additional Qualifications

SEARCH AND RESEARCH

In scouting out keywords to use in your Summary of Qualifications, look at the various postings on websites for your particular job objective. What keywords are used over and over again? You may also want to look up your job objective in the *Occupational Outlook Handbook* at www.bls.gov/oco to see what sorts of keywords are used in the job description. Try to integrate these words into your summary.

CHAPTER 6 / CHECKLIST

In today's market a Summary of Qualifications can help your resume stand out and get noticed. Although optional, it is usually a good idea to include it in your resume. You can use it to:

→ Bring your major accomplishments and employer benefits to the front of the resume where they belong.

→ Use it to stress transferable skills which may be important for your present job objective.

→ Stress personality traits and a strong work ethic which can set you apart from other applicants.

→ List honors, professional affiliations, certificates, and licenses that may be crucial to your job.

→ Stress special skills such as computer skills or language skills (bilingual) that you feel your employer should immediately be aware of.

→ Be selective. It should be a summary—a bird's eye view of your resume. Most importantly, write it with impact.

WORKSHEET INSTRUCTIONS

If your resume warrants a Summary of Qualifications, select five or six of your most outstanding qualifications.

Select this information from your:

1. Unique skills or combination of skills in your Skill List (Chapter 2).
2. List of achievements in your Professional Experience section (Chapter 7 or 8).
3. Outstanding educational achievements in your Education section (Chapter 9).
4. Special awards, honors, or special training (Chapter 10).
5. Total years of experience in the field (only if it is an impressive number).
6. Outstanding personality traits in your Skill List (Chapter 2).

- Write each statement with punch—concise and directly to the point.
- Make sure your statements are results oriented.
- Use action verbs to describe your achievements.
- Highlight keywords whenever possible.
- Reread the section on action verbs in Chapters 7 and 8.

Copy your summary exactly as you want it to appear on your resume to the worksheet page that follows.

RESUME STYLE GUIDELINES

Highlight each statement of your summary with a bullet. In the examples on the previous pages, notice how the bullet (•) made each statement stand out. You can also use a check (✓) or an em-dash (—). The purpose is to distinguish your summary.

CHAPTER 6 / WORKSHEET

SUMMARY OF QUALIFICATIONS

SUMMARY OF QUALIFICATIONS:

1. _____

2. _____

3. _____

4. _____

5. _____

6. _____

PROFESSIONAL EXPERIENCE— CHRONOLOGICAL

A summary of your employment history

In a chronological resume this includes:

- dates of employment (month, year)
- name of the company or organization you worked for
- description of the organization (if necessary)
- location of the company (city and state)
- job title(s)
- responsibilities and duties
- accomplishments, results of these accomplishments, and demonstrated skills

List all past employment, beginning with your most recent employer. Document your work experience by listing your duties and tasks. Demonstrate your ability to contribute by emphasizing your accomplishments and skills.

☑ Excellent
☐ Very good
☐ Good
☐ Average

Prepare to Succeed >>>

This chapter is geared for those who have chosen to use the Chronological Format for their resume. Refer back to the chart on page 33 to see if this is the preferred format for your job search. While the Chronological Resume has been the most traditional format and the one that most employers prefer, in today's market of frequent job changes, the Functional and Hybrid formats are becoming more acceptable in all areas of the workforce. Students who have little real-world experience should opt for the functional style. **If you have settled on using the Functional Format you should skip this chapter and proceed to the next chapter on the Functional and Hybrid Resume Format.**

If you do choose to utilize the Chronological Format, it is best to prepare your information in advance. Be sure you have a list of all your previous jobs, including your exact job title(s), employer(s) and the months and years of your employment. You may want to prepare a timeline to be sure every year is accounted for. You will also want to list each job skill, benefit, and achievement, as well as your major responsibilities on each job. If you have too much information, you may have to be selective and decide which information is the most important and relevant to your present job objective. Select the information that will most impress your future employer.

Demonstrate that you have the experience and the ability to do the job.

YOUR PROFESSIONAL EXPERIENCE IS THE HEART OF YOUR RESUME

Employers will focus on this section of your resume. They will be looking for reasons to eliminate you. Avoid giving them cause for alarm; accentuate positive qualifications and accomplishments.

Demonstrate that you have the experience and the ability to do the job. Prove that you are someone who can solve problems and contribute significantly.

JOB HOPPING AND GAPS IN EMPLOYMENT CAN BE A RED FLAG

The first thing many employers look at on a resume is the "Professional Experience" section in order to spot job hopping or large gaps in the applicant's employment history. Below you will see ways to camouflage these gaps, but rest assured they will be discovered sooner or later and if you make it to the interview stage you will be asked to fill in those gaps or explain why you have changed jobs so often. If you have a good reason, you may want to stress it in a cover letter that you send with your resume. But be sure in all cases you are prepared to explain job hopping and large gaps of time in your job history.

HOW TO PRESENT YOUR INFORMATION

DATES OF EMPLOYMENT

➝ Employers expect to see your dates of employment, and they will check your resume for time gaps. List both the month and year you began working and the month and year your employment ended (or write "until present" if you are still

THE INSIDE SCOOP

"A large gap of unemployed time on a resume can be a red flag. In cases where there is a child involved or someone going back to school, I understand that and usually give the person the benefit of the doubt. Sometimes, I will do a phone interview to find out the reason for a gap. Right off the bat, if there is a lot of job hopping the resume goes right into the 'denial file.'"

Christopher Townsend, Assistant Vice President,
Retail Sales Manager, Royal Banks of Missouri

working at the job). If you indicate only the years, employers may suspect a gap. Conversely, listing more than the month is unnecessary. Short gaps of a few weeks are expected.

↪ If you have gaps that you want to camouflage, you have two choices. You can list your dates of employment after you have listed the company's name and location. (See the Example on page 73.) Listing it at the end detracts attention. Or, you may choose to list *only* the years of employment. This is not ideal, though; resort to it if you have no other choice.

↪ If you held many part-time jobs and do not want to look like a job hopper, consolidate them into one heading such as: 2008–Present: Part-time Employment.

COMPANY'S NAME, DESCRIPTION, AND LOCATION

↪ List the company name. If it is a large corporation, add the division in which you worked. For example: AT&T—Computer Division. If the company is a subsidiary of a larger, more prestigious corporation, mention that as well. For example: Films Classics, Inc., a division of Paramount Pictures Corporation.

↪ If your past employer is not well known (or is not local), you should write a one-line description of the company so that potential employers will get an idea of the type and size of the corporation for which you have worked. For example: Metro Group, a local retail clothing chain with yearly sales in excess of $2 million. Managing a local chain store is significantly different than managing a small "mom-and-pop" outfit. An employer understands the level of your responsibilities by understanding the type of organizations for which you have worked. The same rule is true for a division. Add a line of description about your division if it is vague.

↪ List the city and state where your past employer is located. Do not mention street addresses or phone numbers. If needed, an interviewer can obtain that information or request it on a job application.

JOB TITLE

↪ Use a generic job title that every employer understands. Avoid such titles as Jr. Data Entry Operator—Level Two. It will probably mean little to anyone outside your former organization. Simply state it as Data Entry Operator.

↪ Choose a job title that reflects your level of responsibility. If you were a secretary who was actively involved in decision making, you may want to represent your job title as Administrative Assistant rather than Secretary.

CAUTION: If you do this, be sure your past employer will support you. If someone checks on you and your former boss tells them you were a secretary and not an assistant, you could jeopardize your chances of getting the job. Be sure to check creative job titles with former employers before using them on your resume.

↪ If you have had more than one job title at the same company, set off each job title. List your total years at the company and the company name at the top. Under it, list each job title separately. Under each job title, list the duties and accomplishments for it. Emphasize upward mobility and increased responsibility with each job.

DUTIES AND RESPONSIBILITIES

↪ List three or four of your major duties. Precede it with a catch-all phrase such as "Duties included…," or "Responsible for…" Always use action verbs.

↪ Mention the people (by job title, not name) you interacted with on the job. For example: "Reported to Vice President of Sales," or "Supervised Four Account Executives."

↪ Do not repeat your responsibilities. If you have had more than one job with similar duties, mention those duties only once. If you did dictation in one job, you should not repeat that information again about another job. The reader will already know you have that skill.

↪ Always show upward mobility. Detail your less important duties on earlier jobs and reserve your most impressive duties for your most recent job.

ACCOMPLISHMENTS

↪ List your most impressive accomplishments first. Be specific. Qualify your accomplishments in terms of money saved or other concrete employer benefits.

↪ Do not tell *how* you achieved your accomplishments. Make the employer interested enough to ask how you did it during an interview.

THE INSIDE SCOOP

"One of the red flags I look for is someone who has worked for only a short time yet claims many accomplishments. I question how someone could achieve so much in such a time frame. Also, when someone claims many achievements, I want to know why they want to leave their former place of work. Sometimes things are fine and they just want to better themselves. But many times there is a 'skeleton in the closet' and I try to dig until I find it."

Geoff Green, VP of Talent Acquisition, Brown Shoe, Inc.

EXAMPLE: **YEARS ARE EMPHASIZED**

PROFESSIONAL
EXPERIENCE:

Feb. 2010 to Present   McNAIR MANUFACTURING, INC., Chicago, IL
                             Shoe manufacturer employing 200+ employees
                             Gross sales for 2010 exceeded $2 million.

                             MANAGER
                             Responsibilities included supervising staff of 12,
                             coordinating advertising and promotions, and training
                             new employees. Reported directly to CEO.
                             • Reduced annual operating costs 5 percent by improving
                               warehouse procedure.
                             • Restructured employee communications program, in-
                               creasing in-house communications efficiency.

                             ASSISTANT MANAGER
                             In charge of developing employee training programs.
                             • Awarded Employee of the Year Award in 2011
March 2001 to Jan. 2008   MAY COMPANY—SHOE DEPARTMENT, Chicago, IL

                             MANAGER
                             Assisted sales staff in developing more effective sales
                             techniques. Oversaw all aspects of the department
                             including inventory, and apprised Senior Management
                             of weekly business activity.
                             • Under my leadership, department sales increased more
                               than 18 percent.

EXAMPLE: **YEARS ARE NOT EMPHASIZED**

EXPERIENCE: <u>Marketing Group</u>, Chicago, IL 2011 to Present

                     ACCOUNT EXECUTIVE
                     Responsible for initiating new advertising accounts.
                     • Acquired a major account (Calco, Inc.) resulting in a
                       12 percent revenue increase.
                     • Conceived of and authored a monthly newsletter to raise
                       clients' awareness of new company services.
                     <u>Whitmer Advertising</u>, Chicago, IL 2008 to 2011

                     JR. ACCOUNT EXECUTIVE
                     Learned all aspects of advertising, including TV and radio
                     sales, print ads, and public relations.

WHAT IF YOU HAVE NO OUTSTANDING ACCOMPLISHMENTS?

If you do not have any outstanding accomplishments, then stress your skills. What if
you have been driving a delivery truck for the last six years? You may feel you have
not achieved anything significant, but you do have qualifications you can emphasize—
namely, your unique *combination* of skills.

Which of your skills are *unique?* As a truck driver, perhaps you have an outstanding driving record. Maybe you have a thorough knowledge of the state's or nation's highways. Whatever job or training you have, you can find unique skills that you have acquired and present yourself with impact.

EXAMPLE: **SKILLS ARE EMPHASIZED**

EXPERIENCE:

2011 to Present: Chicago Metro Delivery, Chicago, IL

DRIVER
- Freight transportation in Chicago area
- Inventory control
- Thoroughly familiar with Chicago and environs
- Impeccable driving record

You can also use your Summary of Qualifications to emphasize skills. Skills such as an impeccable driving record or "familiarity with the Chicago region" could also be listed in your Summary. However, do not list them twice. If you list them in your Summary, do not list them again in your Professional Experience. Mentioning the same facts repeatedly gives the impression of padding your resume and will only hurt your chances.

List any outstanding character or personality traits pertinent to the job you seek in your Summary. In the previous example, adding a trait such as "dependable and hard working" would enhance the resume. Again, if you can back these up with facts all the better. For example you could state: "dependable and hard working which led to a promotion in 2012."

The goal is to present yourself with impact. Show that you are someone who takes action and gets things done. Thus, even if you do not have particular outstanding achievements, you can still emphasize your skills in your Summary of Qualifications and Experience sections.

You will now proceed to write your Professional Experience. First, we will explain how to bring your resume to life using action verbs.

ACTION VERBS

WHAT ARE ACTION VERBS AND WHY MUST YOU USE THEM?

Action verbs demonstrate action and results. They are concise and focused, and they enliven a resume.

For example, assume you started a new program to train employees. You could simply state, in very dull terms: "Started a new program to train employees." Or you could state the same information with impact: "Initiated an employee-training program." Notice the difference. The term "initiated" is active and focused. Other suitable action terms here are "created and implemented" or "developed." These words emphasize action—action on your part to get the job done.

However, this example still lacks something. It lacks results. Why does your new program matter? What did it accomplish for your employer?

Whenever possible, connect action verbs with results. If the result of your new program was that employees were trained in three days instead of four, you could write: "Initiated new employee training program that cut training time 25 percent." What if

THE INSIDE SCOOP

"When I give my resume writing seminars, I like to illustrate the use of 'resume action verbs' with this somewhat humorous example: A woman who worked at a fast food enterprise as a dishwasher was preparing her resume. I asked her if she could think of a situation where she saved the company money. She told me that one time the restaurant hired a short order cook who was not familiar with the high-powered equipment in the kitchen. He was about to light the pilot with the gas turned all the way up—which may have caused an explosion and destroyed the kitchen. She immediately stopped him and showed him how that particular oven had to be lit. I jokingly told her that if she chose the right words, she could make a good impression on a future employer. She could describe her 'accomplishment' with the following comment—and every word is true:

Identified a hazardous situation in the workplace and implemented an on-the-spot training program which saved the company thousands of dollars.

Using the right resume jargon and action verbs can add extra significance to what may otherwise be perceived as a menial achievement."

one of your duties was to purchase office supplies? You could simply state the facts: "In charge of purchasing office supplies." However, it would be more effective to highlight the skills you used. You probably searched for the best price and may have even negotiated for lower prices. If so, write with impact: "Evaluated vendors and negotiated for the best prices on all office supplies." The benefit to the employer (the fact that you got the best price, which saved him or her money) is obvious.

Use action verbs anytime you describe your duties, accomplishments, or qualifications.

WHICH ACTION VERBS BEST DESCRIBE *YOUR* ACCOMPLISHMENTS?

The following list, sorted by skill area, will help you find the right action verbs to describe your accomplishments. If your job was one that required managerial skills, the action verbs that describe your task(s) will likely be under that heading.

Most jobs require a combination of skills. Check *all* skill areas that apply to you. Take note of verbs that might qualify, and describe your duties and accomplishments.

Often, multiple words are serviceable. For example, if your job required you to write reports, you could choose any of the following action verbs: wrote, authored, compiled, composed, edited, organized, or designed. They are all effective. Deciding which best describes your accomplishments is your preference.

Action Verbs are the Key to an Effective Resume Because They

- create impact and enliven a resume.
- emphasize action and accomplishments.
- present you as an achiever and a success.
- concisely focus the reader's attention on your accomplishments.

ACTION VERBS—CATEGORIZED BY SKILL AREAS

Creative

authored
conceived
created
designed
developed
devised
directed
enhanced
established
formulated
illustrated
improved
initiated
introduced
invented
launched
marketed
originated
planned
prepared
produced
proposed
set up
structured
wrote

Clerical and Research

arranged
automated
budgeted
calculated
catalogued
classified
collected
compared
compiled
completed
computed
critiqued
decreased
diagnosed
dispatched
distributed
evaluated
examined
executed
generated
identified
implemented
inspected
interpreted

interviewed
investigated
monitored
operated
organized
prepared
processed
purchased
recorded
retrieved
reviewed
scheduled
screened
summarized
surveyed
systematized
tabulated
validated
verified

Human Resources

advised
assessed
assisted
clarified
coached
collaborated
consulted
counseled
diagnosed
educated
employed
grouped
guided
handled
hired
integrated
mediated
monitored
motivated
negotiated
recruited
represented
sponsored
strengthened
trained

Management and Leadership

administered
analyzed
assigned

attained
authorized
chaired
consolidated
contracted
controlled
coordinated
delegated
developed
directed
enacted
established
evaluated
exceeded
executed
expanded
guided
headed
implemented
improved
incorporated
increased
initiated
instituted
investigated
launched
led
maintained
managed
mediated
negotiated
organized
oversaw
performed
planned
prioritized
produced
proposed
recommended
reduced
repositioned
retained
reviewed
revised
scheduled
sorted
strengthened
supervised

Technical

assembled
built
calculated

computed
designed
engineered
operated
overhauled
programmed
remodeled
repaired
solved
upgraded

Financial

allocated
analyzed
appraised
audited
balanced
budgeted
calculated
computed
forecasted
managed
marketed
planned
projected
tabulated

Teaching

advised
clarified
coached
communicated
encouraged
evaluated
explained
guided
influenced
informed
instructed
interpreted
lectured
persuaded
stimulated
trained

Communication

addressed
arbitrated
arranged
authored
convinced
corresponded

developed
directed
drafted
edited
enlisted
formulated
influenced
interpreted
interviewed
lectured
moderated
negotiated
participated
persuaded
presented
presided
promoted
publicized
recruited
represented
sold
spoke
translated
wrote

Success Words

accomplished
awarded
corrected
diverted
eliminated
expanded
generated
identified
improved
masterminded
pioneered
rectified
solved
strengthened
surpassed
turned around
was promoted to
was responsible for

WORKSHEET INSTRUCTIONS

JOB TITLE

On the following worksheet pages, you will write your work experience. On the first page, list your most recent job. On the following pages, list any prior jobs, always mentioning your more recent employment first. (Four worksheets have been provided. If you need more, you may duplicate the worksheet for your use.)

IF YOU HAVE HELD MULTIPLE JOBS AT THE SAME COMPANY:

Devote a separate page to each job title. List the total years you have worked for that company on the first page. On the remaining worksheets, leave this information blank. However, make the notation "same as previous page" so that when you type your resume, you will remember that all the job titles should be under the same employer heading.

IF YOU HAVE HELD MORE THAN FOUR JOBS:

Add extra pages, and follow the same format. Preferably, limit your work experience to four jobs. If you have held many jobs in a short span of time, you will look like a job hopper. Consolidate those jobs into one title such as Part-time Employment, or list only your last four jobs.

DUTIES

What did you do on a daily basis? List your most important tasks first. Use action verbs and stress your skills. Indicate your level of responsibility, such as who you reported to and how many employees you managed. *Above all, be concise!* Do not list more than four duties.

ACCOMPLISHMENTS

Mention important projects on which you worked. Stress your contribution. What compliments did you receive from your boss or coworkers? What have you done that improved the company or saved it money? These are all guidelines for analyzing your accomplishments.

Emphasize all accomplishments in terms of benefits to the employer.

Benefits include:

- Saving money
- Increasing profits
- Lowering unit costs
- Solving emergency situations
- Streamlining operations
- Improving employee relations

- Decreasing costs
- Increasing efficiency
- Eliminating waste
- Expanding client base
- Introducing a new product
- Improving working conditions

Be specific. Give numbers and percentages if possible.

If you made no *major* contributions, stress your skills and skill areas.

RESUME STYLE GUIDELINES

Use bullets for emphasis to distinguish your list of duties and accomplishments.

PROFESSIONAL EXPERIENCE—CHRONOLOGICAL

BE SURE TO FILL OUT *BOTH SIDES* OF THIS SHEET.

PROFESSIONAL EXPERIENCE:

JOB TITLE—MOST RECENT JOB:

_____

DATE EMPLOYMENT BEGAN (Month, Year):   DATE TERMINATED (or "to Present"):

_____, 20 _____   _____

NAME OF EMPLOYER/COMPANY/ORGANIZATION AND DEPARTMENT (if company is large):

_____

EMPLOYER'S ADDRESS (City, State):

_____

_____

_____

DESCRIPTION OF THE COMPANY OR DEPARTMENT (if the company is not well-known):

_____

_____

_____

(continued)

CHAPTER 7 / WORKSHEET (CONTINUED)

PROFESSIONAL EXPERIENCE—
CHRONOLOGICAL

DUTIES AND RESPONSIBILITIES:

List three or four of your daily tasks and duties.

(Begin with the catchphrase: "Responsible for/Responsibilities included/Duties included." Bullet [•] each duty for emphasis.)

_____

_____

_____

_____

_____

_____

_____

ACCOMPLISHMENTS OR MAJOR SKILLS:

List four or five. Bullet [•] each for emphasis.

_____

_____

_____

_____

_____

_____

_____

_____

CHAPTER 7 / WORKSHEET

PROFESSIONAL EXPERIENCE— CHRONOLOGICAL

BE SURE TO FILL OUT *BOTH SIDES* OF THIS SHEET.

PROFESSIONAL EXPERIENCE:

JOB TITLE—MOST RECENT JOB:

_____

DATE EMPLOYMENT BEGAN (Month, Year):   DATE TERMINATED (or "to Present"):

_____, 20 ____ - _____

NAME OF EMPLOYER/COMPANY/ORGANIZATION AND DEPARTMENT (if company is large):
_____

EMPLOYER'S ADDRESS (City, State):
_____
_____
_____

DESCRIPTION OF THE COMPANY OR DEPARTMENT (if the company is not well-known):
_____
_____
_____

(continued)

CHAPTER 7 / WORKSHEET (CONTINUED)

PROFESSIONAL EXPERIENCE— CHRONOLOGICAL

DUTIES AND RESPONSIBILITIES:

List three or four of your daily tasks and duties.

(Begin with the catchphrase: "Responsible for/Responsibilities included/Duties included." Bullet [•] each duty for emphasis.)

_____

_____

_____

_____

_____

_____

ACCOMPLISHMENTS OR MAJOR SKILLS:

List four or five. Bullet [•] each for emphasis.

_____

_____

_____

_____

_____

_____

_____

_____

CHAPTER 7 / WORKSHEET

PROFESSIONAL EXPERIENCE—CHRONOLOGICAL

BE SURE TO FILL OUT *BOTH SIDES* OF THIS SHEET.

PROFESSIONAL EXPERIENCE:

JOB TITLE—MOST RECENT JOB:

_____

DATE EMPLOYMENT BEGAN (Month, Year):   DATE TERMINATED (or "to Present"):

_____ _____, 20 ____   _____

NAME OF EMPLOYER/COMPANY/ORGANIZATION AND DEPARTMENT (if company is large):

_____

EMPLOYER'S ADDRESS (City, State):

_____

_____

_____

DESCRIPTION OF THE COMPANY OR DEPARTMENT (if the company is not well-known):

_____

_____

_____

(continued)

CHAPTER 7 / WORKSHEET (CONTINUED)

PROFESSIONAL EXPERIENCE— CHRONOLOGICAL

DUTIES AND RESPONSIBILITIES:

List three or four of your daily tasks and duties.

(Begin with the catchphrase: "Responsible for/Responsibilities included/Duties included." Bullet [•] each duty for emphasis.)

_____

_____

_____

_____

_____

_____

_____

ACCOMPLISHMENTS OR MAJOR SKILLS:

List four or five. Bullet [•] each for emphasis.

_____

_____

_____

_____

_____

_____

_____

_____

CHAPTER 7 / WORKSHEET

PROFESSIONAL EXPERIENCE— CHRONOLOGICAL

BE SURE TO FILL OUT *BOTH SIDES* OF THIS SHEET.

PROFESSIONAL EXPERIENCE:

JOB TITLE—MOST RECENT JOB:

_____

DATE EMPLOYMENT BEGAN (Month, Year):   DATE TERMINATED (or "to Present"):

_____ , 20 _____   _____

NAME OF EMPLOYER/COMPANY/ORGANIZATION AND DEPARTMENT (if company is large):

_____

EMPLOYER'S ADDRESS (City, State):

_____

_____

_____

DESCRIPTION OF THE COMPANY OR DEPARTMENT (if the company is not well-known):

_____

_____

_____

(continued)

CHAPTER 7 WORKSHEET (CONTINUED)

PROFESSIONAL EXPERIENCE— CHRONOLOGICAL

DUTIES AND RESPONSIBILITIES:

List three or four of your daily tasks and duties.

(Begin with the catchphrase: "Responsible for/Responsibilities included/Duties included." Bullet [•] each duty for emphasis.)

_____

_____

_____

_____

_____

_____

ACCOMPLISHMENTS OR MAJOR SKILLS:

List four or five. Bullet [•] each for emphasis.

_____

_____

_____

_____

_____

_____

_____

_____

PROFESSIONAL EXPERIENCE— FUNCTIONAL

A summary of your skill areas and employment history

In a Functional Resume this includes:

- headings that emphasize skill areas
- job responsibilities, duties, and accomplishments organized according to the skills they use
- skills and accomplishments primarily emphasized over job titles or periods of employment

In a hybrid resume you would also include:

- a list of employers and job titles, and optionally, dates of employment

☑ Excellent
☐ Very good
☐ Good
☐ Average

Prepare to Succeed >>>

This chapter is aimed at those who have chosen to use the Functional Format for their resume. Refer back to the chart on page 83 to make sure this is the preferred format for you. **If you have chosen this format, you should have skipped the previous chapter on Chronological Format.** You will begin composing your employment history in this chapter.

While the chronological resume has been the most traditional format and the one that most employers prefer, in today's market of frequent job changes, the functional and hybrid formats are becoming more acceptable in all areas of the workforce. This is particularly true for students and recent graduates who have little real-world experience. They usually find it in their best interest to opt for the functional style. Also, the functional format can help mask job hopping that would be clearly obvious on the chronological format. Those returning to work after a long hiatus as well as those who fear age discrimination will also find the pure functional format preferable.

However, be warned. There is no getting away from revealing your past work history chronologically. Even if you chose a pure functional format and you eliminate your dates of employment, you can be certain the employer will ask you for a detailed account either in your interview or on a job application. Therefore as you prepare your functional format resume, it is a good idea to have a list of the dates, job titles, and past employers on hand for easy reference.

For this resume format, focus on major skill headings you possess that are most relevant for the job at hand. You will want to choose two or three major skill headings. Sometimes two related skills can be combined, such as "Advertising and Promotions" or "Marketing and Sales." Be able to support each skill heading with two or three examples from you work history that demonstrate to an employer that you have indeed mastered those skills.

If you are trying out for different jobs with different objectives, just as you will want to compose a separate resume for each individual objective, you will also want to rearrange your skill headings so that the first skill listed is also the main skill required for each individual objective. Remember, always put your most relevant and impressive information first.

EMPHASIZE YOUR SKILLS

The functional resume is particularly effective if you have limited experience in the workplace or if you are changing jobs. The functional format will focus the employer's attention on your skills rather than your limited experience or, if you have continuously changed jobs, your numerous employers.

LIST YOUR DUTIES AND STRESS YOUR ACCOMPLISHMENTS

In the functional resume you list your work experience just as you do in the chronological resume. The difference is in the presentation. In the chronological format, everything is listed according to the job title and employer. In a functional format, all similar qualifications are organized under the same skill heading, regardless of where or when they were performed.

For example, if you worked for McCormick Public Relations and were in charge of print ads for two years and then took a job with another agency and were in charge of print ads and radio for three years, you would list all of these skills under one heading. You might use the headline Advertising and list all of your advertising experience underneath.

Rol   chke/Shutterstock.com

Include any skill an employer would be impressed with in your resume.

SEARCH AND RESEARCH

To choose the best skill headings you may have to do some research. Besides the charts in Chapter 2, you may find it easier to employ the skill headings that are used in the job listings. Researching your job title objective online may also unearth some useful skill headings. As mentioned many times before, the Department of Labor's *Occupational Outlook Handbook* website (www.bls.gov/oco) may be helpful. The main goal is to choose only those headings that are relevant and important for your specific job objective, and to limit them to no more than three.

You might also check out how others in your field have presented their skills and skill areas by looking at their LinkedIn profiles.

In this case you might write: "More than five years of print ad experience. Demonstrated ability to coordinate print and radio advertising." If you also did clerical work while at McCormick, you would list that under another headline—Clerical or perhaps Administrative Skills.

BE CONCISE

This rule holds true regardless of the format you choose. Limit your skill headings to three at maximum. If you have more, consolidate them. For example, as mentioned above you might combine Advertising and Public Relations into one heading.

Choose only those skill headings that support your objective. If you are looking for a job as an accountant, you would want to use headings such as Accounting or Budgeting, rather than Teaching or Motivational Training. Be selective and choose *only* skill areas that interest your employer.

THE HYBRID RESUME

One of the best features of the functional resume is that it lets you choose which skills you want to emphasize. The downside is that many employers expect to see a chronological resume, and when they don't, they worry that you are exaggerating your skills or, worse, that you are hiding something. Moreover, employers want to see the names

SUCCESS STORY

Sid C. was a retired litigation lawyer who decided he wanted to become a teacher in his spare time. Because his previous work experience had been exclusively in law, he knew that a chronological style resume stressing his law experience would not get much notice. Instead he chose to do a functional format. Since in his law practice he was successful in captivating and swaying a jury, Sid figured he could use those public speaking skills and do the same with high school students. His knowledge of law and U.S. history were certainly strong enough to teach high school. By stressing his public speaking skills, his ability to engage his listeners, as well as his impeccable knowledge of law and history, Sid soon found himself being interviewed for high school teaching positions for both Business Law and American Constitution. In no time, Sid was hired and became one of the most popular teachers at his high school.

of your past employers. Knowing the type of organizations you have worked for helps them understand the responsibilities you can handle, as well as the quality of the work they can expect from you.

Therefore, even if you choose a functional format, it is best to include a short summary of your past employers. This format is often referred to as a "hybrid resume" as it integrates the major strengths of both resume formats. While it emphasizes your skill areas it still touches on your past employment history, briefly summarizing past job titles, as well as the name and location of your previous employment. If you have a solid history, you should mention the dates of employment as well. However, do not mention your duties or accomplishments, because you have already listed them under your skill areas.

The following example is for someone whose objective is Sales. Note that only sales-related skill headings are used. In a classic functional resume, the employment history section would be omitted.

The following example is a hybrid format with employment history summarized.

EXAMPLE: **HYBRID FORMAT**

MARKETING & SALES
- Sold custom designed fixtures and standard display products
- Researched and developed target market and leads
- Expanded client base to include major corporations
- Organized local trade shows

PROMOTION & ADVERTISING
- Implemented promotional giveaway program that increased sales 12 percent
- Designed successful advertising materials
- Developed point-of-purchase displays for the company's six stores
- Researched and selected local trade publications to place ads with greatest cost efficiency

EMPLOYMENT HISTORY

Sales Manager
Jerry's Fixtures, St. Paul, MN—Largest fixtures chain in the St. Paul area

Sales Associate
Sunshine World, St. Paul, MN

ACTION VERBS

WHAT ARE ACTION VERBS AND WHY MUST YOU USE THEM?

Action verbs demonstrate action and results. They are concise and focused, and they enliven a resume.

For example, assume you started a new program to train employees. You could simply state, in very dull terms: "Started a new program to train employees." Or you could state the same information with impact: "Initiated an employee-training program." Notice the difference. The term "initiated" is active and focused. Other suitable action terms here are "created and implemented" or "developed." These words emphasize action—action on your part to get the job done.

THE INSIDE SCOOP

"When I give my resume writing seminars, I like to illustrate the use of 'resume action verbs' with this somewhat humorous example: A woman who worked at a fast food enterprise as a dishwasher was preparing her resume. I asked her if she could think of a situation where she saved the company money. She told me that one time the restaurant hired a short order cook who was not familiar with the high-powered equipment in the kitchen. He was about to light the pilot with the gas turned all the way up—which may have caused an explosion and destroyed the kitchen. She immediately stopped him and showed him how that particular oven had to be lit. I jokingly told her that if she chose the right words, she could make a good impression on a future employer. She could describe her 'accomplishment' with the following comment—and every word is true:

Identified a hazardous situation in the workplace and implemented an on-the-spot training program which saved the company thousands of dollars.

Using the right resume jargon and action verbs can add extra significance to what may otherwise be perceived as a menial achievement."

However, this example still lacks something. It lacks results. Why does your new program matter? What did it accomplish for your employer?

Whenever possible, connect action verbs with results. If the result of your new program was that employees were trained in three days instead of four, you could write: "Initiated new employee training program that cut training time 25 percent." What if one of your duties was to purchase office supplies? You could simply state the facts: "In charge of purchasing office supplies." However, it would be more effective to highlight the skills you used. You probably searched for the best price and may have even negotiated for lower prices. If so, write with impact: "Evaluated vendors and negotiated for the best prices on all office supplies." The benefit to the employer (the fact that you got the best price, which saved him or her money) is obvious.

Use action verbs anytime you describe your duties, accomplishments, or qualifications.

WHICH ACTION VERBS BEST DESCRIBE *YOUR* ACCOMPLISHMENTS?

The following list will help you find the right action verbs to describe your accomplishments. The key verbs are sorted according to skill areas. If your job was one that required managerial skills, the action verbs that describe your task(s) will likely be under that heading.

Most jobs require a combination of skills. Check *all* skill areas that apply to you. Record verbs that could qualify and describe your duties and accomplishments.

Often, multiple words are serviceable. For example, if your job required you to write reports, you could choose any of the following action verbs: wrote, authored, compiled, composed, edited, organized, or designed. They are all effective. Deciding which best describes your accomplishments is your preference.

Action Verbs Are the Key to an Effective Resume Because They

- create impact and enliven a resume.

- emphasize action and accomplishments.

- present you as an "achiever" and a "success."

- concisely focus the reader's attention on your accomplishments.

ACTION VERBS—CATEGORIZED BY SKILL AREAS

Creative

authored
conceived
created
designed
developed
devised
directed
enhanced
established
formulated
illustrated
improved
initiated
introduced
invented
launched
marketed
originated
planned
prepared
produced
proposed
set up
structured
wrote

Clerical and Research

arranged
automated
budgeted
calculated
catalogued
classified
collected
compared
compiled
completed
computed
critiqued
decreased
diagnosed
dispatched
distributed
evaluated
examined
executed
generated
identified
implemented
inspected
interpreted

interviewed
investigated
monitored
operated
organized
prepared
processed
purchased
recorded
retrieved
reviewed
scheduled
screened
summarized
surveyed
systematized
tabulated
validated
verified

Human Resources

advised
assessed
assisted
clarified
coached
collaborated
consulted
counseled
diagnosed
educated
employed
grouped
guided
handled
hired
integrated
mediated
monitored
motivated
negotiated
recruited
represented
sponsored
strengthened
trained

Management and Leadership

administered
analyzed

assigned
attained
authorized
chaired
consolidated
contracted
controlled
coordinated
delegated
developed
directed
enacted
established
evaluated
exceeded
executed
expanded
guided
headed
implemented
improved
incorporated
increased
initiated
instituted
investigated
launched
led
maintained
managed
mediated
negotiated
organized
oversaw
performed
planned
prioritized
produced
proposed
recommended
reduced
repositioned
retained
reviewed
revised
scheduled
sorted
strengthened
supervised

Technical

assembled
built

calculated
computed
designed
engineered
operated
overhauled
programmed
remodeled
repaired
solved
upgraded

Financial

allocated
analyzed
appraised
audited
balanced
budgeted
calculated
computed
forecasted
managed
marketed
planned
projected
tabulated

Teaching

advised
clarified
coached
communicated
encouraged
evaluated
explained
guided
influenced
informed
instructed
interpreted
lectured
persuaded
stimulated
trained

Communication

addressed
arbitrated
arranged
authored

convinced
corresponded
developed
directed
drafted
edited
enlisted
formulated
influenced
interpreted
interviewed
lectured
moderated
negotiated
participated
persuaded
presented
presided
promoted
publicized
recruited
represented
sold
spoke
translated
wrote

Success Words

accomplished
awarded
corrected
diverted
eliminated
expanded
generated
identified
improved
masterminded
pioneered
rectified
solved
strengthened
surpassed
turned around
was promoted to
was responsible for

W O R K S H E E T   I N S T R U C T I O N S

The following four practice worksheets should prepare you for writing a functional or hybrid resume. The first step in writing a functional resume is to choose your Skill Headings. This can be complicated. We usually think in concrete terms (what tasks we performed) rather than thinking in the abstract (what skills we used). These practice worksheets should help you analyze which skills or skill areas you used most often.

On the practice worksheets, enter your employment history in chronological order, beginning with your last job. List your job title, employer, and dates of employment. If you choose a traditional functional format, this information will not appear in your resume. However, documenting it will focus you.

Next, list your three major duties and three major accomplishments for each job. Then, on the line to the right of each duty and accomplishment, list the skill or skills that you used for that job.

For example, if you kept books, took dictation, and did word processing, your list might look like this:

1. <u>Bookkeeping</u>   <u>Financial and clerical skills</u>

2. <u>Dictation</u>   <u>Clerical Skills</u>

3. <u>Word Processing</u>   <u>Computer and Clerical Skills</u>

In this example, the tasks could all be listed together under one heading: CLERICAL. Alternatively, they could each be listed under separate headings: Bookkeeping under FINANCIAL, Dictation under CLERICAL, and Word Processing under COMPUTER. Decide based on which major skill areas you want to emphasize.

Review the charts in Chapter 2. Items in the list of Technical Skills can be Skill Headings. The list of Skill Areas and Specific Tasks will also help.

After you have compiled a list from your last four jobs, check the skill areas you have listed. The ones that appear the most are your *major skill areas*.

From these major skills, which ones are the most relevant to the job you are presently seeking?

The skill areas that fulfill both requirements (major skill areas and those that are most relevant to your Career Objective) are the Skill Headings you will use in your resume. Choose the three most impressive headings.

There are three final worksheets for skill headings; you will devote one page to each skill heading.

Under each heading, list the three or four most impressive duties and accomplishments that you performed with that skill. Finding that information should be easy. Check the right-hand column for the skill, and then look at the task associated with it.

These worksheets enable you to compose quickly and accurately a functional resume.

If you want to use the hybrid format, add your list of job titles and employers (and optionally, your periods of employment) on the last worksheet page of this chapter under Employment History. That information should also be easy to find—copy it from the top portion of your worksheets.

If you have too many major skill areas, consolidate them. Combine two similar skills into one heading, such as Publicity and Advertising or Marketing and Sales. Additionally, if one task involves two skills (word processing involves both Computer Skills and Clerical Skills), choose the one that best corresponds with your career goal.

USE ACTION VERBS

Review the list on page 93 and use it as an aid in describing your duties and accomplishments.

CHAPTER 8 / WORKSHEET

PROFESSIONAL EXPERIENCE PRACTICE

JOB TITLE: _____

NAME OF EMPLOYER: _____

EMPLOYER'S CITY AND STATE: _____

DATES OF EMPLOYMENT (Month, Year):

From: _____, 20_____ to _____, 20_____

THREE MAJOR DUTIES OR RESPONSIBILITIES:

1. _____

_____

2. _____

_____

3. _____

_____

SKILLS USED:

_____

_____

_____

_____

_____

_____

THREE MAJOR ACCOMPLISHMENTS:

1. _____

_____

2. _____

_____

3. _____

_____

SKILLS USED:

_____

_____

_____

_____

_____

_____

CHAPTER 8 WORKSHEET

PROFESSIONAL EXPERIENCE PRACTICE

JOB TITLE: _____

NAME OF EMPLOYER: _____

EMPLOYER'S CITY AND STATE: _____

DATES OF EMPLOYMENT (Month, Year):

From: _____, 20_____ to _____, 20_____

THREE MAJOR DUTIES OR RESPONSIBILITIES:

SKILLS USED:

1. _____

_____

2. _____

_____

3. _____

_____

THREE MAJOR ACCOMPLISHMENTS:

SKILLS USED:

1. _____

_____

2. _____

_____

3. _____

_____

CHAPTER 8 WORKSHEET

PROFESSIONAL EXPERIENCE PRACTICE

JOB TITLE: _____

NAME OF EMPLOYER: _____

EMPLOYER'S CITY AND STATE: _____

DATES OF EMPLOYMENT (Month, Year):

From: _____, 20_____ to _____, 20_____

THREE MAJOR DUTIES OR RESPONSIBILITIES:

SKILLS USED:

1. _____   _____

    _____   _____

2. _____   _____

    _____   _____

3. _____   _____

    _____   _____

THREE MAJOR ACCOMPLISIIMENTS:

SKILLS USED:

1. _____   _____

    _____   _____

2. _____   _____

    _____   _____

3. _____   _____

    _____   _____

CHAPTER 8 / WORKSHEET

PROFESSIONAL EXPERIENCE PRACTICE

JOB TITLE: _____

NAME OF EMPLOYER: _____

EMPLOYER'S CITY AND STATE: _____

DATES OF EMPLOYMENT (Month, Year):

From: _____, 20_____ to _____, 20_____

THREE MAJOR DUTIES OR RESPONSIBILITIES:

1. _____

_____

2. _____

_____

3. _____

_____

SKILLS USED:

_____

_____

_____

_____

_____

_____

THREE MAJOR ACCOMPLISHMENTS:

1. _____

_____

2. _____

_____

3. _____

_____

SKILLS USED:

_____

_____

_____

_____

_____

_____

WORKSHEET INSTRUCTIONS

FUNCTIONAL FORMAT

Complete the following worksheet pages exactly as you want them to appear on your resume.

Fill in your skill heading at the top of each worksheet.

Under each skill heading, list four or five qualifications that fall under that particular skill.

Qualifications can be either duties and responsibilities or accomplishments. Limit yourself to five maximum.

You should also compare your worksheets with your Skill Sheet (Chapter 1). Additionally, reviewing the skill lists in Chapter 1 should help you avoid omitting an important skill.

- Use action verbs to describe your skills and accomplishments.
- Do not repeat information.
- Be concise.

HYBRID FORMAT

Complete the last page, too. The heading is Employment History. List your past job titles, employers, location of employment, and, if you have a solid work history, your time periods of employment.

RESUME STYLE GUIDELINES

Emphasize qualifications and duties with bullets before each statement.

CHAPTER 8 / WORKSHEET

PROFESSIONAL EXPERIENCE— FUNCTIONAL

PROFESSIONAL EXPERIENCE:

Skill Heading _____

LIST FOUR OR FIVE MAJOR DUTIES AND/OR ACCOMPLISHMENTS:

(Use bullets in front of each statement.)

1. _____

   _____

   _____

2. _____

   _____

   _____

3. _____

   _____

   _____

4. _____

   _____

   _____

5. _____

   _____

   _____

CHAPTER 8 / WORKSHEET

PROFESSIONAL EXPERIENCE— FUNCTIONAL

PROFESSIONAL EXPERIENCE:

Skill Heading _____

LIST FOUR OR FIVE MAJOR DUTIES AND/OR ACCOMPLISHMENTS:

(Use bullets in front of each statement.)

1. _____

    _____

    _____

2. _____

    _____

    _____

3. _____

    _____

    _____

4. _____

    _____

    _____

5. _____

    _____

    _____

    _____

CHAPTER 8 WORKSHEET

PROFESSIONAL EXPERIENCE— FUNCTIONAL

PROFESSIONAL EXPERIENCE:

Skill Heading _____

LIST FOUR OR FIVE MAJOR DUTIES AND/OR ACCOMPLISHMENTS:

(Use bullets in front of each statement.)

1. _____
_____
_____

2. _____
_____
_____

3. _____
_____
_____

4. _____
_____
_____

5. _____
_____
_____
_____

CHAPTER 8 / WORKSHEET

PROFESSIONAL EXPERIENCE—FUNCTIONAL

PROFESSIONAL EXPERIENCE:

JOB TITLE: _____

NAME OF EMPLOYER: _____

EMPLOYER'S CITY AND STATE: _____

DATES OF EMPLOYMENT (Month, Year):

From: _____, 20_____ to _____, 20_____

JOB TITLE: _____

NAME OF EMPLOYER: _____

EMPLOYER'S CITY AND STATE: _____

DATES OF EMPLOYMENT (Month, Year):

From: _____, 20_____ to _____, 20_____

JOB TITLE: _____

NAME OF EMPLOYER: _____

EMPLOYER'S CITY AND STATE: _____

DATES OF EMPLOYMENT (Month, Year):

From: _____, 20_____ to _____, 20_____

JOB TITLE: _____

NAME OF EMPLOYER: _____

EMPLOYER'S CITY AND STATE: _____

DATES OF EMPLOYMENT (Month, Year):

From: _____, 20_____ to _____, 20_____

EDUCATION

Highest level of education achieved (highest degree), graduation date, university or college attended, city, state

- Add special recognitions, achievements (high GPA), scholarships, awards, and any other highlights of your education (majors, minors, special courses), if the information is relevant to your career objective.

- Mention professional training, workshops, seminars, and other informal education relevant to your objective here, too.

- Conversely, if you have worked for three or more years, highlight your present accomplishments, and reduce the emphasis on education. In this situation, you would position Education after Professional Experience.

- **FOR RECENT GRADUATES:** Position this section immediately after your Objective or Summary of Qualifications and before the Professional Experience heading. Because your actual employment experience will be limited, you will want to place extra emphasis on your education, detailing projects and achievements relevant to your career objective.

☑ Excellent
☐ Very good
☐ Good
☐ Average

Prepare to Succeed >>>

For the recent graduate, the "Education" section of the resume may be the most important. Since most graduates have yet to work full time, their major skills and experience may be limited to what they have studied in school and the projects they have completed in their classroom. Employers understand that students may not have real-life work experience, but they also understand that school can be a microcosm of the workplace with deadlines, decision making, projects, and creativity duplicating real working conditions. If one can succeed in school, chances are he or she will succeed at work. That's why it's important to play up any and all of the accomplishments, awards, and outstanding work you have achieved during your time at school. Letters of recommendations from your teachers and professors can also make a difference. While many of these items will not be included in your resume, it is a good idea to keep a file with all the letters, outstanding work, and projects you may want to bring with you to the interview. If your education is your experience, be sure to give this section everything you've got!

The more real work experience one gains with time, the less critical it is to mention this education experience. If someone has already had a full time job in the real world, the Education section will follow the Employment History as its importance will have become secondary.

Photodisc/Getty Images

Mention professional training, workshops, seminars, and other informal education relevant to your objective here, too.

YOUR EDUCATION IS RELEVANT!

Your education is important to your employer for two reasons. First, education equals skills. Employers will translate your education into skills you have acquired. They want people with skills that can help them. Indicate any areas of study, professional workshops, or special projects that display a skill area beneficial to an employer. Second, a university setting is similar to the workplace. A successful student, one with a high GPA or one who excelled in other areas, has ambition and drive—traits essential to succeeding in the workplace. A successful student will be a successful employee.

Remember this and add any educational highlights that reflect your skill and expertise, as well as all accomplishments that demonstrate your ability to succeed. If you have other professional training, such as workshops or seminars, list them.

Even if you lack an outstanding educational history, do not omit this section. Obtaining a college degree is an accomplishment that most employers look for. If you do not have a college background, indicate that you did graduate high school. Many jobs do not require more than a high school education, and the employer will want to be sure that you have at least earned your high school diploma.

If you mention your college degree, mentioning your high school diploma is unnecessary. However, list any other college degrees—B.A., M.A., and so forth. Begin with your last degree (or the degree you are presently working on). Use a reverse chronology and mention your other degrees or training.

If you supported yourself during college, you may add that fact. You might even state: "Earned 35 percent of my college expense" (or whatever percentage). This displays qualities that employers seek in an employee—initiative and drive.

EXAMPLE: **EDUCATION—RECENT GRADUATE**

EDUCATION:	**M.B.A. Business Administration, 2012** University of Florida—Miami Beach, FL • Major: Financial Management • Emphasis on Financial Forecasting • Dean's List 2009–2012 • GPA 3.50/4.00 • Tuition paid via part-time employment as financial advisor • President of Future Business Leaders of America, 2007 **B.A. Economics, 2008** University of Illinois—Chicago, IL

EXAMPLE: **EDUCATION—EMPLOYEE WHO GRADUATED SOME YEARS AGO**

EDUCATION:	**M.B.A. Business Administration, 2012** University of Florida—Miami Beach, FL Major: Financial Management **B.A. Economics, 2011** University of Illinois—Chicago, IL Participated in weeklong seminar (Fall 2010): "Financial Forecasting" with Martin Shanks. Mastered more accurate methods for forecasting.

Notice the difference in these examples. The recent graduate details areas of expertise (emphasis on financial forecasting). Additionally, the recent graduate mentions such success indicators as Dean's List and a 3.50 GPA. Furthermore, the fact that the student paid tuition through work as a financial advisor is included. Employers will be impressed with this initiative and even more so with the use of college skills while gaining field experience.

The employee who graduated some years ago should not overemphasize education. Even mentioning a major is unnecessary, although it strengthens the resume if the objective is a job in finance. Mentioning the seminar is important because the employee gained a valuable skill (more accurate forecasting methods) that will benefit the employer.

Always tell employers what they want to hear: that your education has equipped you with skills and qualifications that will benefit their organization.

STRESS YOUR LEADERSHIP QUALITIES AND OTHER IMPORTANT TRAITS

One of the qualities that employers look for is a candidate who shows leadership abilities and those who have initiative. While there are obviously no educational courses to teach these qualities, you can demonstrate that you indeed possess these important traits. Taking part in professional associations says a lot about your personality. Don't forget to stress any extracurricular involvement, volunteer work or otherwise that demonstrates your initiative to go beyond what is expected. Notice how in the above example of a recent graduate, being president of an extracurricular club was added. These activities do carry weight and should never be overlooked in your resume.

THE INSIDE SCOOP

"One of the things I look for when hiring is how a candidate interacts with others, which reveals key personality traits. How they interacted in school is important, as is their ability to lead and take initiative. Leadership and getting along with others are strong indications of their personality."

Christopher Townsend, Assistant Vice President, Retail Sales Manager,
Royal Banks of Missouri

W O R K S H E E T   I N S T R U C T I O N S

Fill out the following practice worksheet.

If you are a college graduate, fill out the first section. You do not need to mention your high school if you have a college degree or are working toward one.

Fill out all the information about your college—even if you are not a recent graduate. Later you will select the information to include in your resume.

You can abbreviate your degree (M.A., B.A., M.B.A., and so forth).

You can abbreviate your grade point average (GPA).

Be sure to list the city and state of your college, university, or high school.

If you are currently seeking a college degree, the degree you are presently working on should come first. You can document it like this:

M.A. Program—Business Administration

UCLA, Los Angeles, CA

Additionally, if you have not yet received your degree, do not mention dates. If the employer wants to know, you can explain during the interview.

If you lack a college degree, complete the section on high school. If you have recently graduated high school (in the last year), you should also complete the section highlighting your high school experience. If you have been working for more than one year, do not include your high school accomplishments. Mentioning your high school and graduation date is sufficient.

If you have trade school or apprenticeship experience, complete the last section on special training. Furthermore, add any workshops, seminars, or special skills you have acquired (such as computer skills) that support your job objective and would benefit the employer.

If your special training skills are crucial to your job and deserve emphasis, you can devote an entire section heading to them.

Following the section on Education, you may add a new category: Special Training. Below this head list all special skills such as computer expertise or other proficiencies that you have acquired through training.

CHAPTER 9   WORKSHEET

EDUCATION PRACTICE

IF YOU HAVE A COLLEGE EDUCATION

WHAT IS THE HIGHEST DEGREE YOU RECEIVED OR ARE PRESENTLY WORKING ON?
_____

WHAT YEAR DID YOU GRADUATE? _____

WHAT COLLEGE OR UNIVERSITY IS YOUR DEGREE FROM?

Name: _____

City: _____ State: _____

YOUR MAJOR (if relevant to your objective): _____

YOUR MINOR (if relevant to your objective): _____

WHAT SPECIAL COURSES OR PROJECTS WOULD INTEREST YOUR EMPLOYER?
1. _____
2. _____
3. _____

WHAT SPECIAL HONORS, ACHIEVEMENTS, OR SCHOLARSHIPS DID YOU RECEIVE?
1. _____
2. _____
3. _____
4. _____

THESIS OR PUBLICATIONS:
1. _____
2. _____

WHAT OTHER DEGREES HAVE YOU RECEIVED? _____

FROM WHICH COLLEGE DID YOU RECEIVE THAT DEGREE?

Name: _____

City: _____ State: _____

YOUR MAJOR (if relevant to your objective): _____

CHAPTER 9 WORKSHEET

EDUCATION PRACTICE

IF YOU *DO NOT* HAVE A COLLEGE EDUCATION

DO YOU HAVE A HIGH SCHOOL DIPLOMA? WHICH HIGH SCHOOL?

Name: _____

City: _____ State: _____

Graduation Date: _____

IF YOU ARE A *RECENT* HIGH SCHOOL GRADUATE

LIST ANY AWARDS OR ACHIEVEMENTS YOU RECEIVED IN HIGH SCHOOL:

1. _____
2. _____
3. _____
4. _____

SPECIAL TRAINING

TRADE SCHOOLS, APPRENTICESHIPS, SEMINARS, WORKSHOPS, ETC.

LIST ANY INFORMAL EDUCATION THAT WOULD INTEREST YOUR EMPLOYER:

1. _____
2. _____
3. _____
4. _____

WORKSHEET INSTRUCTIONS

Follow the guidelines below to select the most impressive information from your practice worksheet. Complete the education section on the following worksheet page exactly as you want it to appear on your resume.

Study the examples within the chapter and notice the format. The degree is bolded and important accomplishments are bulleted (•). You could use underlining, all caps, or even italics instead of boldface.

SELECTING THE MOST IMPRESSIVE INFORMATION

IF YOU ARE A COLLEGE GRADUATE:

1. Begin with your most recent degree. Include your area of study. Do not write B.A.; rather B.A. Psychology. On the same line, put your year of graduation.
   Two Exceptions:
   - ➶ If you graduated long ago, omit the date.
   - ➶ If you took time off after college before working and the employer will notice a gap in your work history, omit the date. If the employer is interested, you can explain the gap during the interview.

On the next line, write the name of the university or college, and on the same line, follow with the school's location—city and state.

Follow this with major areas of study, if relevant to your career objective:

B.A. Psychology, 2010

University of Southern California—Los Angeles, CA

Emphasis on Counseling and Abnormal Psychology

IF YOU ARE A RECENT GRADUATE:

1. List any important achievements, student activities, honors, and so forth that are relevant to your objective or demonstrate your ability to succeed. Emphasize this information with bullets.

IF YOU HAVE BEEN IN THE WORKPLACE FOR MORE THAN TWO YEARS:

1. Mention only those scholastic areas that will translate into skills for your employer. Accomplishments, GPA, and scholarships lose their importance the longer you have been out of school.

2. List any other *major* degrees, such as an undergraduate degree. Do not mention junior college if you have graduated from a university or college. Follow the same procedure in listing your other degrees, but decrease the emphasis on these less recent accomplishments and areas of study.

3. List any special graduate or informal training that you have received in workshops, seminars, or night school. Skip a line after your degree and university before listing any special training. Otherwise, it will appear as though you received this training at the university.

IF YOU ARE NOT A COLLEGE GRADUATE:

1. Mention your high school and follow it with your year of graduation. Follow the exception above for when to omit your graduation date. On the next line, follow with the city and state of your high school.

   Rogers High School, 2012
   Chicago, IL

2. If you are a *recent graduate* follow the above rule for recent college graduates, listing relevant accomplishments, areas of study, and student activities.

3. Skip a line and list any special skills that you have acquired since high school, and where you acquired them (workshop or apprenticeship).

CHAPTER 9 WORKSHEET

EDUCATION

EDUCATION:

_____

_____

_____

_____

_____

_____

_____

_____

_____

_____

_____

ADDITIONAL QUALIFICATIONS

The end of your resume is a good place to highlight additional qualifications and credentials that you could not fit elsewhere

Additional qualifications include:

- honors and awards
- publications
- membership in professional organizations
- licenses and accreditations
- fluency in foreign languages
- computer skills
- web design
- digital photography
- special skills
- civic involvement / volunteer work
- military record
- hobbies, if relevant to your objective
- speaking engagements
- short testimonial blurbs

☑ Excellent
☐ Very good
☐ Good
☐ Average

Prepare to Succeed >>>

The Additional Qualifications section is great for highlighting important information that may either be lost in the body of your resume or may not relate directly to any of the other headings. If you are highlighting a variety of items that are unrelated, this heading will be labeled "Additional Qualifications." However, if you are mainly listing certificates or honors or perhaps computer skills, you may opt for a more specific heading such as "Certificates and Professional Associations" or "Computer Skills." The more specific you can be, the more effective the information will be.

VITAL INFORMATION THAT BELONGS IN YOUR RESUME

If the job at hand requires specific certificates, it is imperative that you list them on your resume. Listing professional associations is also an excellent idea. With the proliferation of many social media sites online, it is easy to become a member of just about any professional association. Being a member of a professional association is important because it demonstrates that you are a person who is interested in keeping up with the latest information and advances in your field.

A side benefit of listing these associations and additional qualifications is that it may, in most cases, be a way to add important keywords to your resume. These keywords can sometimes make the difference in your resume being selected from the hundreds of others that are being considered.

Listing Additional Qualifications in your resume can help you stand out in other ways as well. Listing published articles or speaking engagements establishes you as an expert in your field. Professional associations and continuing education courses demonstrates that you are someone who is continually learning and interested in all advances in your field. Listing volunteer work and civic associations can show off important character traits such as leadership, compassion, and having an ethical and social conscience. These personality traits are sometimes more important to an employer than technical skills that you can learn on the job.

Recently, some applicants have added brief testimonial quotes from past employers. However, one should be leery of hyperbole and be very cautious of adding these quotes. Employers will check your references and if you exaggerate about what your references have said about you, it will make you look untruthful and set off a red flag. If you are interested in informing a future employer of what past employers have to say

Listing volunteer work and civic associations can show off important character traits such as leadership, compassion, and having an ethical and social conscience.

about you, it would be best to have them compose letters of recommendation which can be attached to the resume or brought to the interview.

Those seeking non-technical jobs can use Additional Qualifications to highlight computer skills and other technical skills that may be important in all areas of today's workforce—not just information technology fields.

Hobbies and interests should be added **only** if they relate to the job to which you're applying. Most employers won't care that you are an expert badminton player or that you enjoy puzzles in your spare time. Every statement on your resume is important and every word should be chosen with care. Don't waste space on statements that are irrelevant.

ONLY LIST QUALIFICATIONS THAT SUPPORT YOUR OBJECTIVE

Most people find it best to use a single heading such as "Additional Qualifications." Underneath, you can list all awards, honors, professional affiliations, and licenses. See Example 1.

If you would rather emphasize each of these, use a separate heading for each. For example, you could use a heading such as Licenses, and under it list the various licenses you have. Below that you could add another heading such as Professional Affiliations, and list under that all of your pertinent affiliations. See Example 2.

It's important to choose only qualifications that correspond to your career objective or demonstrate your ability to succeed. If you are applying for a job as a banker, do not mention your membership in a ham radio club. However, that membership would interest an employer if you are seeking a job in radio and communications.

If you have multiple awards or memberships, you should use bullets to draw attention to them. See Example 1.

EXAMPLE 1:

ADDITIONAL QUALIFICATIONS:	• Fluent in French and Spanish • Member of International Law Associates • Frequent contributor to *Law Week*

EXAMPLE 2:

LICENSES & PROFESSIONAL AFFILIATIONS:	• 1st Class FCC License • Ham Radio Operators of North America • Vice President, Radio Broadcasters of America (Since 2009)

THE INSIDE SCOOP

"Sometimes so many applicant resumes have the same education, course training, and skills that it becomes difficult to choose who to bring in for an interview. This is especially true with recent graduates who still have little real-world employment experience. Many times only after reading their Additional Qualifications can I decide which applicants I want to bring in. In many instances it is this little bit of extra information that makes them stand out. Professional associations are important to me, as is most volunteer work. Things that show me leadership qualities and a strong work ethic are also very important.

"One thing many applicants don't realize is that they should avoid any volunteer work that is associated with religious or political organizations. All volunteer work listed should be generic or non-denominational. While I would like to say that no one is prejudiced in today's work market, the brutal truth is that in the real world prejudice does exist. Even if it is on a subconscious level, it is unfortunately a reality of life. Someone can be eliminated from an interview simply by stating on his or her resume that he or she did volunteer work for the Republican Party, if the interviewer is a Democrat. You must be careful what goes on your resume. Don't leave yourself open to prejudice."

—Melvin Zuhler, President, American Eyewear Center

SEARCH AND RESEARCH

Search online to discover which professional associations apply to your profession. Just search "professional associations" and "your profession or professional field"—for example "professional associations & psychologists." Most of these associations' websites will have instructions on how to become a member. Social media networks such as LinkedIn offer members a choice of groups to join. Also you can ask your LinkedIn contacts and others in your profession which associations are important and how to join.

W O R K S H E E T   I N S T R U C T I O N S

Decide how you want your additional information presented. If you want to emphasize multiple areas, such as honors and special training, decide if you want everything under one heading, such as Additional Information, or under two headings, such as Honors and Special Training.

If your additional information consists solely of honors, use that as your heading.

Do not overdo it; use no more than two additional headings. Otherwise, you draw attention away from the rest of your resume.

Complete the following worksheet page exactly as you want your additional qualifications to appear on your resume.

Look at the list of headings from the beginning of the chapter. Choose your heading or headings.

1. Write the heading(s).
2. List qualifications that are pertinent to that heading. If you have more than two qualifications under one heading, you should use bullets to emphasize and distinguish them.

CHAPTER 10 WORKSHEET

ADDITIONAL QUALIFICATIONS

HEADING #1: _____

QUALIFICATIONS: _____

_____

_____

_____

_____

_____

_____

_____

HEADING #2: _____

QUALIFICATIONS: _____

_____

_____

_____

_____

_____

_____

_____

_____

REFERENCES

☑ Excellent
☐ Very good
☐ Good
☐ Average

Prepare to Succeed >>>

Almost every employer today wants to see references and will check them carefully—but they do not need or want to see them on your resume. You will be asked at some point to supply references, though. It is important that you not only limit your references to three persons, but you must be cautious to select only those persons you are certain will give you a glowing recommendation. And be sure your references are industry people and not relatives.

In this chapter, you will prepare a separate References document that you will bring with you to the interview or, if asked, attach to your resume. Be sure you contact your references ahead of time and let them know they may receive a call from a future employer about you, and be sure to send them a copy of your resume to keep them up to date on your accomplishments. References today are a must; be sure you are prepared.

EVERY EMPLOYER CHECKS REFERENCES

Due to the hyperbole found on many of today's resumes, employers have become more skeptical and as a result are even more diligent when checking references. However, due to today's increasing number of applicants and resumes, employers rarely have time to check every applicant's references before they are interviewed. Thus, you need not put your references on your resume. However, you can be certain that after you have been brought in for an interview and you are a running candidate, an employer will call and check your references. Employers want to be certain that you actually achieved, or have the talent to achieve, the accomplishments that you boast about on your resume. That's why you will need to prepare a references document to bring with you to the interview. This one-page document should match your resume's letterhead and should list no more than three references with phone numbers and addresses.

Many times, letters of recommendation are even more important than the references themselves. If you have a truly outstanding letter of recommendation it should certainly be included with your resume. Any letters of recommendation you've received should also be brought with you to the interview. Be sure the letter contains the writer's name, job title, and phone number or e-mail address so that the employer

Lisa F. Young/Shutterstock.com

Employers will check references to be certain you have the skills you've listed on your resume.

can contact him or her if the employer wants to verify the letter. Employers do verify letters and references, especially for advanced jobs that require higher levels of expertise and trust. In some jobs employers may even ask for a polygraph test to verify your honesty. However, in many states and for many jobs this has become a legal issue and as a result many employers have dropped the polygraph tests. As a result, they are giving more and more attention to the references their applicants supply.

If you have many letters of recommendation, you may consider making a mock "press sheet" in which you select short phrases and testimonial statements from a few of the letters and place the quotes (with names and phone numbers) all on one sheet of paper. This acts as an ad, allowing the employer to see the highlights of many letters at once. It can be very effective. Of course, always keep the original letters in case the employer asks to see them as well.

Keep in mind that if you don't have a reference page, most employers will ask you to fill out some sort of application in which you will be required to list your references. One way or another, you will have to provide this list.

One other point of particular importance: Be sure to contact your references first and inform them they may be called. It should go without saying that you should never have a reference who might have anything negative to say about you or give you a less-than-glowing report. Be selective.

REFERENCES AVAILABLE UPON REQUEST— NO LONGER NECESSARY

In the past, adding "References—Available on Request" at the end of a resume was customary. Today, it is unnecessary. Employers expect every applicant to have solid references. If you believe that you have exceptional references and want to direct the employer's attention to them, you may increase interest by writing "Excellent references available on request." The word *excellent* may raise the employer's interest, but be sure you can deliver those outstanding references.

Never assume your reference will automatically give you a good recommendation, as many may not remember your accomplishments the same way you do. Therefore, call your references on the phone first. Ask them if they will give you a good recommendation and if you can use them as references. Remind them of your past accomplishments, and update them on your present status. Moreover, send each a copy of your resume so that he or she has it nearby if an employer calls. Do not rely on a reference's memory. If an employer asks a reference about your accomplishments and he or she cannot remember, you will look bad and it may jeopardize your chances of being hired.

Your list of references should resemble your resume. It should have your contact information on your letterhead. The term **REFERENCES** should follow in bold letters, all caps, and be centered. Underneath, list your references. Be sure to give full names, job titles, company names, companies' complete addresses, and phone numbers. Make it easy for the employer to contact your references. Study the example on the next page to see how to format your reference list. A sample format sheet follows on page 138.

1. Call your references and make sure they will give you good recommendations.

2. Send each a copy of your resume to review. It will remind and update them on your qualifications.

THE INSIDE SCOOP

"When I hire someone to run a vending route, the two most important things I look for are: 'Are they trustworthy?' and 'Are they dependable?' These qualities are more important to me than any of their so-called 'skills.' Before the laws changed, I used to administer polygraph tests, but I can't do that anymore. Now I pay very close attention to their references. Not only do I check out the references they supply, but as a rule I always call their last employer even if they they're not listed as a reference. In this business I have to take every precaution."

C.L. – Owner, Snacks-R-Us Vending

EXAMPLE:

REFERENCES

MELISSA BRODY
Sr. Vice President, Sales
Micro-Technics Computers
6787 North State Street
Des Moines, IA 90000
(555) 989-0098

POSTING YOUR RECOMMENDATIONS ON LINKEDIN

One of the most useful tools that LinkedIn offers is a section where you display your recommendations prominently. While these recommendations are taken exclusively from your LinkedIn contacts, if your have a recommendation from someone outside your network, you can always ask them to join. Because they come from co-workers and past employers, these recommendations are very important, especially today when most hiring managers will Google you and view your LinkedIn profile (or anything else found online). In your cover letter you will want to direct employers to your LinkedIn page where they can check out your recommendations. You can also print out your recommendations from LinkedIn and bring the hard copy with you to the interview, the same way you might bring any other letter of recommendation.

If you maintain your own website where you have posted your resume, you can post your recommendations there as well. You can even link your references to the References Available heading of your web resume. You may want to use a password to protect this page, if you want it seen only by preferred persons. In presenting your website references, you should follow all the previous instructions and include all the relevant information, in case an employer wants to contact any of them. Be sure that your references do not mind being a part of your website.

THE INSIDE SCOOP

"Today, I rarely check references before an interview unless I happen to personally know the reference or someone from that company. But I do always search online for the person and see what is out there in cyberspace on him or her. In this way I do my own research and 'references' on that person."

Geoff Green, VP of Talent Acquisition, Brown Shoe, Inc.

W O R K S H E E T   I N S T R U C T I O N S

On the worksheet page, list your references *exactly* as you want them to appear on your final reference list.

On each succeeding line, enter

- ↱ your reference's full name (add Mr. or Ms. if the gender is questionable)
- ↱ his or her position (job title)
- ↱ his or her company (full name)
- ↱ the company's address (include the suite number if applicable)
- ↱ the city, state, and zip code
- ↱ your reference's area code/phone number/extension

Make it easy for your potential employer to reach your references.

RESUME STYLE GUIDELINES

Emphasize your references' names with boldface letters. You may even want to bold both their names and positions. This is especially appropriate if your reference person is well known or holds a powerful and highly respected position.

You may also consider centering your references and setting each off with a bullet (•) between them. (See the sample resumes in Chapter 12.)

Look at the example on page 138. Use the same paper stock (color and quality) as your resume.

Again, be sure your letterhead (contact information) appears on your reference list. Thus, if your reference list becomes separated from your resume, your employer will still know whose contacts these are.

EXAMPLE: **SAMPLE REFERENCE SHEET**

ANDRE WALKER

1212 Sutton Drive
Mountain Top, NY 90000
(555) 882-8789

REFERENCES

•

Tim O'Conner
Vice President Computer Operations
MacGraphics International
1334 Old Ridge Road
Wilton, OH 90000
(555) 897-0098

•

Ms. Yun-Ming Lee
Executive Vice President
Sealico Steel & Metal
700 Sparrow Lane
Tiger Creek, AK 90000
(555) 877-8768

•

Yolanda Haskins
Creative Director
Mountain Top Advertising
987 Winchester Plaza
Suite 865
Mountain Top, NY 90000
(555) 897-8700

CHAPTER 11 WORKSHEET

REFERENCES

1. _____

(name)

_____

(job title)

_____

(company)

_____

(address—street/suite number)

_____

(city, state, zip)

_____

(area code/phone number)

2. _____

(name)

_____

(job title)

_____

(company)

_____

(address—street/suite number)

_____

(city, state, zip)

_____

(area code/phone number)

3. _____

(name)

_____

(job title)

_____

(company)

_____

(address—street/suite number)

_____

(city, state, zip)

_____

(area code/phone number)

PUTTING IT ALL TOGETHER

Prepare to Succeed >>>

The Sequence of Your Resume Headings

Now that you've completed the text of your resume, you must put it all together. There are two steps in putting your resume together: The first step is placing your resume headings and text in their proper order and sequence. The second and perhaps more important step is formatting and printing your resume with an eye-catching, professional looking layout.

In this chapter, you will organize your worksheets in the proper order, edit them, and finally write your final resume draft. After you have your draft in front of you, you will choose the best layout and fonts that will produce a stand-out resume.

ORGANIZING YOUR RESUME HEADINGS AND TEXT

As mentioned previously, the order of the resume headings and text should follow this simple rule of thumb: Your most important and pertinent information appears first and always precedes the less important information. Thus your last job title precedes your previous jobs. If you are a graduating student, your education and degree will be more significant than your work experience and will thus precede it. In your Summary of Qualifications your most impressive accomplishments should come first.

Unless you are applying for a job in the arts or a creative field, stick with traditional fonts that are clean and easy to read, such as: Palatino, Century Gothic, Century School-book, Arial, or Bookman. Many programs by default use Times New Roman. While this is an excellent font, it is perhaps overused and choosing one of the other fonts may help your resume stand out. Never mix fonts. However, you may choose a different font (and even a more artistic one) for your letterhead and contact information, to make it stand out from the rest of your resume text. Never use a font size smaller than 10, and try to stick with a 12-point font if you can. Readability is your primary concern. Use good paper, 20-25 lb., that measures the standard 8½x11-inches. Most office supply and copy stores carry special higher quality resume paper. Don't skimp on the paper and printing. Again, be professional every step of the way.

Last but not least, be sure to check and double check your spelling. You don't want to have printed out a hundred copies on expensive paper only to find you have misspelled words or transposed numbers in your phone or address information.

iofoto/Shutterstock.com

Readability is your primary concern.

Once you have double checked all your worksheets, you are ready to put your resume together. Be sure you have finished your Summary of Qualifications, which should have been completed last. Detach all of the worksheet pages, and place them in the proper sequence.

Your Contact Information is your letterhead and should come first.

Next is your Objective. If you believe the inclusion of an objective will limit your probabilities of getting many different types of jobs, you may omit it. However, as pointed out previously, most experts recommend including an objective or career goal. The objective will enhance your prospects of getting the job you want. Furthermore, with the increasing practice of information filing, you often need an objective to identify yourself for the proper job. If personnel is unsure what job you are applying for, your resume will be trashed rather than filed. If you want to apply for a broader job area, tell your employer about the other types of work you are willing to do in your cover letter.

Your Summary of Qualifications belongs next. This is optional. Use it if you have unique or outstanding qualifications that you want your employer to see immediately.

If you are a recent graduate, your Education section comes next, followed by your Professional Experience if you have any.

If you are not a recent graduate, your Professional Experience (chronological or functional format) comes next. In a functional-hybrid format you follow your Professional Experience with a short employment summary under the heading: Employment History. This is then followed by your Education.

End with any pertinent information such as Awards and Professional Affiliations.

If you have space remaining on the page, you can end with the proverbial "References Available on Request," although this is not required.

SEARCH AND RESEARCH

To see sample resumes in your career field, you can Google 'sample resumes' and your job title. For example: 'accountant and sample resume' will turn up a variety of websites displaying sample resumes for accountants. LinkedIn is also a good place to view sample resumes. On the LinkedIn home page you can do a search on your job title to find members in your career field. You'll discover that most members have linked their resumes to their profile page. Viewing resume samples online will not only help you in formatting and wording your resume, but can even make you aware of important information you may have omitted.

FORMATTING YOUR RESUME

Remember, you want to project a professional image to ensure that your resume will get noticed. No one will read a messy resume, with clusters of words and long paragraphs staring at them. You need an eye-catching layout. This means short sentences with substantial white space. It also means using bullets, caps, underlining, italics, and boldface to emphasize important information. If you do not have a word processing program with a top-notch printer, take your resume to a printing service. Most copy shops will do the job for a reasonable price, and this is money well spent.

Check the sample resumes that follow to get an idea of an easy-to-read, inviting layout.

Print at least 50 copies of your resume on a good stock of paper such as one with linen or laid finish. The best color for a resume is off-white, eggshell, or gray. Ask the printer for samples of resume paper and choose one with an executive look.

Before you print your resume, complete the checklist that follows. After you have put your resume together, use this checklist to rate your resume. If your resume has problems, fix it before you spend money printing it.

Furthermore, have someone who does not know you well read your resume. What image does it project to a stranger? Is it accurate? Have you included all the necessary information neatly, concisely, and correctly? If so, you have a solid resume. Additionally, have a friend proofread your resume. Sometimes another person will notice flaws that you overlooked.

THE INSIDE SCOOP

"When considering a candidate, we always take into consideration how they actually write their information. Do they leave out capitals, or misspell words? Are they articulate on paper? Do they use proper grammar? In other words, are they making the effort to make themselves look professional?"

—*Stephanie Yaffee, President, TLC for Kids, Nanny & Child Care Services*

Resume Checklist

☐ My Contact Information is complete and correct.

☐ My e-mail address is included.

☐ My Objective is clearly defined.

☐ My resume is concise (no longer than two typed pages).

☐ My irrelevant personal information is excluded.

☐ My responsibilities and accomplishments are described by action verbs.

☐ My benefits to an employer are emphasized throughout.

☐ My image is that of a problem solver.

☐ My major accomplishments have all been mentioned.

☐ My accomplishments are described with concrete examples (supported by numbers or percentages).

☐ My resume format corresponds with my career goal.

☐ My past employers and job tasks are clear.

☐ My layout is eye-catching, with margins, indents, and headings that make it easy to read.

☐ My information is highlighted and emphasized with bullets.

☐ My paper stock is good, and off-white or gray in color.

☐ My resume presents a positive image of me!

☐ My resume projects a professional image!

TO WRITE AND FORMAT ELECTRONIC RESUMES (E-RESUMES), SEE CHAPTER 16.

EXAMPLE: **SKILLED WORKER WITH NO FORMAL EDUCATION—CHRONOLOGICAL FORMAT**

MICHAEL THOMPSON

7988 North Brooks Road
Chicago, IL 90000
(555) 544-0987

OBJECTIVE

DRIVER/TRANSPORTATION MANAGER—where my extensive experience as a professional driver of straight trucks, my ability to train and supervise a driving crew, and my knowledge of warehouse management will be utilized to more efficiently run a transportation operations company.

PROFESSIONAL QUALIFICATIONS

- Outstanding driving record
- Thorough knowledge of the Chicago area
- Excellent physical condition—able to load heavy freight and operate lift gate
- Dependable, hardworking
- Always maintains good rapport with customers

EXPERIENCE

2012 to Present

<u>Chicago Metro Delivery Service, Inc.</u>, Chicago, IL
DRIVER
Freight transportation in Chicago and surrounding environs
Supervised crew of five
Completed all invoices and standard order forms

2009 to 2012

<u>Sugarette Delivery</u>, Chicago, IL
DRIVER
Transporting materials throughout Illinois
Responsible for inventory control

2007 to 2009

<u>Metro-plex, Inc.</u>, Willmette, IL
ASSEMBLER
Assembly line—automotive vehicles
Repair work

LICENSES & CERTIFICATES

- Class 2 License
- D.O.T. License

REFERENCES

Excellent references available upon request

EXAMPLE: RECENT GRADUATE—CHRONOLOGICAL FORMAT

MARIA HERNANDEZ
Route 343
Nashville, TN 90000
(555) 989-8765
mhernand@juno.com

CAREER OBJECTIVE
Psychological Counselor for group or individual counseling in a hospital or rehabilitation center where my counseling experience combined with my sensitivity toward patients will result in superior handling of patients' needs.

EDUCATION
B.A. Psychology, 2006—University of Missouri, St. Louis, MO
- Emphasis on:
  — Clinical Problems in Childhood
  — Adolescent Psychology
  — Abnormal Psychology
  — Industrial and Organizational Psychology
- GPA 3.5 (4.0 in major)
- Dean's List—all four years
- Tuition paid via part-time employment, including working as a Psychological Counselor

PROFESSIONAL EXPERIENCE

Sept. 2009
to Present

VICTIMS SERVICE COUNCIL, Clayton, MO

Phone Counselor
- Provided victims of crime with moral support via outreach phone calls
- Assisted victims with food, medical, and counseling referrals

June 2006
to
June 2009

CAMP WYATT, Springfield, IL
Camp for Underprivileged/Emotionally Disturbed Youths

Unit Director (Summer 2008)
- Promoted from Counselor to Unit Director
- Trained and evaluated 15 counselors
- Designed and conducted workshops for counselors on camp procedures

Counselor (Summer 2007)
- Worked with six- and seven-year-olds who required special attention in building social skills/self-esteem
- Worked with senior citizens

FOREIGN LANGUAGES
Fluent in Spanish—reading and writing

EXAMPLE: **E-RESUME FOR MARIA HERNANDEZ (***SEE CHAPTER 16 FOR MORE DETAILS.***)**

MARIA HERNANDEZ
126 Sampson Street
Nashville, TN 90000
Phone: 555-989-8765
mhernand@gmail.com

KEYWORD SUMMARY

Psychological counselor, group counseling, individual counseling, phone counselor, hospital, rehabilitation center, adolescent psychology, abnormal psychology, industrial psychology, organizational psychology, senior citizens, youths, crime victims, emotionally disturbed, crisis center, Bachelor of Arts, Psychology, dean's list, Spanish, sensitive, empathetic

CAREER OBJECTIVE

Psychological Counselor for group or individual counseling in a hospital or rehabilitation center where my counseling experience combined with my sensitivity toward patients will result in superior handling of patients' needs.

EDUCATION

B.A. Psychology, 2012—University of Missouri, St. Louis, MO
- Emphasis on:
  — Clinical Problems in Childhood
  — Adolescent Psychology
  — Abnormal Psychology
  — Industrial and Organizational Psychology
- GPA 3.5 (4.0 in major)
- Dean's List—all four years
- Tuition paid via part-time employment, including working as a Psychological Counselor

PROFESSIONAL EXPERIENCE

Jan. 2013–Present

PHONE COUNSELOR—Victims Service Council, Clayton, MO
- Provided victims of crime with moral support via outreach phone calls
- Assisted victims with food, medical, and counseling referrals

June 2011–2013

UNIT DIRECTOR & COUNSELOR—Camp Wyatt, Springfield, IL

Camp for Underprivileged/Emotionally Disturbed Youths
- Unit Director (Summer 2012)
  — Promoted from Counselor to Unit Director
  — Trained and evaluated 15 counselors
  — Designed and conducted workshops for counselors on camp procedures
- Counselor (Summer 2011)
  — Worked with six- and seven-year-olds who required special attention in building social skills/self-esteem
  — Worked with senior citizens

FOREIGN LANGUAGES

Fluent in Spanish—reading and writing

EXAMPLE: RESUME FOR A MEDICAL ASSISTANT

MAHOGANY B. MAKESHA – MEDICAL ASSISTANT
8712 Green Meadow Court • Dogsville, California • 90058
(555) 555-1235
mmakesha@gmail.com
• • • • • • • • • • • • • • • • • • •

OBJECTIVE:
A highly talented **Medical Assistant** with more than seven years experience in performing patient screening, collecting, handling, and processing patients' laboratory specimens, including phlebotomy and performing routine in-house laboratory tests; administering medications to patients on specific orders from a provider as well as medical clerical duties.

SUMMARY OF QUALIFICATIONS
- Experience of more than seven years as a Medical Assistant.
- Uncommon ability to apply common sense understanding to carry out instructions furnished in written, oral, or diagram form.
- Strong ability to communicate effectively and clearly (both written and oral communication).
- Remarkable ability to interact effectively with other employees in all levels of the organization as well as with the general public.
- Excellent knowledge of clerical and computer skills like Word, Excel, Outlook, and Access. Exceptionally good demonstration and communication skills both orally and written. Great manual dexterity; ability to reach above the shoulder level to work; bend, squat, sit, stand, stoop, crouch, reach, kneel, twist, and turn.
- Demonstrated ability to work in a busy clinic and multi-program environment.

PROFESSIONAL HISTORY:
Medical Assistant
Our Lady of Spain Clinic, Dogsville, CA
2009-present
- Responsible for the measuring signs such as temperature, pulse rate, weight, height, blood pressure, etc., and interviewing patients to record their information.
- Gave treatment and injections to patients and also performed the routine tests in laboratory.
- Responsible for the keeping records like x-ray reports and schedule appointments, receiving bills, etc.
- Maintained the data of the patients and office and keep the records, billing, transactions, books, etc.
- Responsible for the sterilizing and cleaning of instruments and preparation of the treatment rooms for patients.

EDUCATION:
Certified Diploma in Nursing, Viola Institute of Medical Studies (2009)
Advanced Diploma in Medication & Aid, Viola Institute of Medical Studies (2011)

EXAMPLE: **CHRONOLOGICAL FORMAT—FUNCTIONAL EMPLOYMENT HISTORY**

KISHA DANIELS
9898 West 54th St.
Rockford, IL 90000
Home: 555-990-0988 • Work: 555-997-0900 • kdaniels@gmail.com

CAREER OBJECTIVE
Metallurgical Engineer in the capacity of **Production Supervisor**—where my extensive knowledge of alloys, my trouble-shooting ability, and my top managerial skills will increase productivity and lower costs.

SUMMARY OF QUALIFICATIONS
- Investigated and solved "stain" problem that Coral, Inc. (company's largest account) experienced with an alloy. My cost-efficient solution kept Coral a satisfied customer.
- Identified and solved serious clogging problem on a Wertli Casting machine, ultimately improving the output of the machine.
- Designed new technique of thin-strip casting that reduced waste and cut production costs by more than 25 percent.

EMPLOYMENT HISTORY
Metallurgical Engineer/Production Supervisor   2001–Present
COBB INDUSTRIES, Rockford, IL

RESEARCH AND DEVELOPMENT
- Assisted Mineral Research Group in testing new materials
- Conducted experiments to establish new products

MANAGEMENT
- Supervised and guided staff of five engineers
- Prepared project costs and time estimates
- Determined equipment and raw materials modifications by maintaining close contact with representatives of equipment suppliers, reducing operating costs by 12 percent

PRODUCTION / TROUBLE-SHOOTING
- Designed and implemented cost-saving D.C. casting technique—still in use today
- Solved major stain problem for preferred customer, Coral
- Identified and solved serious mineral clogging problem on Wertli Casting machine

EDUCATION
Masters of Science—Metallurgy, 2000
University of Michigan, Detroit, MI

Associate Degree—Mining Technology
Haileybury School of Mines, Ontario, Canada
Areas of Study: Surveying and Extractive Metallurgy

SEMINARS & WORKSHOPS
- *Management by Objectives*—two-week workshop by Jake Peters, Ph.D., 2002
- *Finance for Nonfinancial Managers*—two-day course, 2006

EXAMPLE: **FUNCTIONAL/HYBRID FORMAT**

DAVID KATIDORIAN

1212 OTTER DRIVE
LOS ANGELES, CA 90000
(555) 889-8789
dkatidor@hotmail.com

PROFESSIONAL OBJECTIVE

SECURITY SYSTEMS TECHNICIAN—where I will utilize my nine years of experience in installing and maintaining alarm and security systems, my expertise and knowledge of diverse control panels and their programming, and my proven ability to repair faulty systems to improve productivity and increase efficiency and profits.

PROFESSIONAL EXPERIENCE

INSTALLATION/SUPERVISION

- Commercial and residential security systems
- Burglar and fire alarm systems—with patrol response
- Analyzed layout for proper placement of security sensors and equipment, eliminating future problems and complaints
- High-quality installations
- Contracted to supervise and check quality control of subcontracted installers and servicers

MAINTENANCE

- Repairing faulty systems
- Locating swinging circuits
- Locating ground circuits

PRODUCT DEMONSTRATION

- Conducted seminars for installers and servicers
  — Demonstrated security equipment and procedures
- Excellent customer communications skills
  — Ability to clearly instruct customers on system's use, thereby reducing future call-ins for assistance

EMPLOYMENT HISTORY

2009–Present   **INSTALLER/TECHNICIAN** (subcontractor)
                      Studio Security, Burbank, CA

2000-2009   **INSTALLER**
                      Bel-Air Patrol, Los Angeles, CA
                      (These L.A. firms service many demanding celebrities)

EDUCATION

Associate of Science Degree, School of Engineering
CAL-CEDA, Reseda, CA

CHAPTER 13

THE COVER LETTER AND OTHER CORRESPONDENCE

☑	Excellent
☐	Very good
☐	Good
☐	Average

Prepare to Succeed >>>

A cover letter is a great way to augment your resume. It can explain away gaps in your employment history, emphasize your skills, and give added details to demonstrate you are the right candidate for the job. Traditionally a cover letter accompanies the resume and works with it to create a total picture of you as the perfect employee.

In this chapter you will be introduced to different forms of cover letters and you will learn to compose an effective cover letter to accompany your resume. You will also be introduced to other important but often overlooked correspondences that should be a part of your job search arsenal as well. Many employers feel the cover letter is equally if not more important than the resume itself and that as much care should go into preparing an effective cover letter.

DIFFERENT TYPES OF COVER LETTERS

There are several different kinds of cover letters of which you should be aware. Each one is designed for a unique situation but all have one common denominator—to get you noticed and land an interview. A few of the most common cover letter formats are:

INQUIRY LETTER (ALSO KNOWN AS A BROADCAST LETTER)

These are letters sent to companies that interest you, but haven't yet advertised job openings. Inquiry letters should contain information on why the company interests you and why your skills and experience would be an asset to them. Be sure to make it clear that you are interested in a job should an opening become available. Be sure to include your contact information as well as how you plan to follow-up.

REFERRAL LETTER

If you have a contact that referred you to a company, or better yet to a hiring manager or recruiter, it's important to mention that person immediately at the start of your letter. Personnel are more likely to give preference to candidates who were referred by someone they know. You should also mention how you know the contact person and your professional connection with them. Even if there is no current opening, managers tend to file away candidates who come with referrals and recommendations.

NETWORKING LETTER

Networking letters can be sent to many of your connections to request job search advice and assistance. These can include letters of introduction, referral letters, letters requesting a meeting, and letters seeking career advice. Not only should these letters be sent to people you know, but they can also be sent to connections to whom you were referred. Networking letters may be sent by mail, e-mail, or even through social media websites such as LinkedIn.

INTERNSHIP LETTER

Send an internship letter to perspective employers or to advertised internship posts to request an interview. Although most internships pay little or nothing, they can supply you with excellent experience and job skills that may be useful in getting your dream job when the time comes. Your letter should make it clear when you are available as well as what skills you can bring to the table. Enclose your resume and contact information as well.

All job search correspondence should match in design and format. Use the same letterhead (and fonts) that you use in your resume, cover letters, and other correspondence. Use the same high-grade paper as your resume and the same font style. However, even if you have to use a 10-point font on your resume, on your cover letter and correspondence you should always use a 12-point font size, as it is the easiest to read and the acceptable standard for all business correspondence. Use an easy-to-read layout (short paragraphs). Most important, check and double check spelling and grammar. Spelling errors such as "I pay close attention to every detale" or "I hope to hear from you shorty" can be embarrassing and may result in your elimination. Every piece of correspondence you send out—even a simple thank-you note—must present you as a professional. When used properly, these letters will not only make you stand out from the crowd, but will also help you get your foot in the door and on your way to the job you want.

PURPOSE OF THE COVER LETTER

Many people think that the cover letter is just a formality and, at best, merely a device to draw the employer's attention to a resume. Consequently, they are content to write a nominal cover letter that simply directs attention to the enclosed resume and asks that it be reviewed. These people are putting their confidence entirely in their resume—and they are making a critical mistake.

The purpose of the cover letter is to make a favorable impression on the employer and to get you an interview. Frequently it is the well-crafted cover letter that gets the applicant an interview, not the resume. In today's market, where employers are more suspect of a resume's validity and integrity, the cover letter is gaining increasing importance. Often, a cover letter can do more than a resume, and the combination of both—a well-crafted cover letter and a strong resume—can give you the edge and the interview.

ELECTRONIC COVER LETTERS (E-COVER LETTERS)

Today, electronic cover letters are becoming common and often replace the standard cover letter reviewed here. In Chapter 16 the rules of writing and formatting an e-cover letter are discussed at length. However, most experts agree that it is essential to arm yourself with a well-executed, detailed cover letter as well.

Many employers will not read any unsolicited e-mail because of the high volume of spam. It is best to contact an employer beforehand to ask if you may send him or

THE INSIDE SCOOP

"Because it is so hard to adequately sum up a person in a one page resume, I like it when I see a cover letter that comes with a resume. Many times the cover letter will give me clearer picture of the person without getting too deep into the resume."

—Christopher Townsend, Assistant Vice President and Retail Sales Manager, Royal Banks of Missouri

her an e-mail or e-resume. Informing them in advance will also increase the chances of your resume being read and selected.

EIGHT THINGS A COVER LETTER CAN DO

1. **State What and Why**
   State exactly *what you can do* for the employer, and *why he or she should hire you*. Your resume is a history of your past, but your cover letter allows you to make a statement about your future. It allows you to specify in exact terms what you plan to do for the employer if you are hired. This requires research on your part. You will have to understand what problems employers are looking to solve and/or how your skills will benefit them. The entire focus of your cover letter should be on the benefits you will bring to the employer.

2. **Make a Personal Connection**
   The resume is an impersonal document, written for a large audience. On the contrary, you can personalize your cover letter. Write each cover letter to a specific company and, most important, directly to the person in charge of hiring. Finding out that person's name and addressing your letter to him or her personally (even if it is just to the head of personnel) can put you ahead of the competition.

3. **Highlight Your Skills and Accomplishments**
   The cover letter can highlight skills and accomplishments that apply directly to the job at hand. By writing to a specific company with particular needs, you can highlight your most appropriate skills and customize each letter to emphasize the information that would most interest the employer to whom you are sending your resume. Ensure that your resume substantiates the skills mentioned in your cover letter. The cover letter should present a glimpse of what you can and will do for the employer, and it should help the employer predict and visualize your success in the job. If an employer can predict your performance better, your chances of getting an interview are greater.

4. **Convey Enthusiasm and a Positive Attitude**
   Your enthusiasm as well as a positive attitude about the company with whom you are seeking employment should come across in your cover lever. You will have to do some homework here. Research the company and show the employers that you know what their organization is doing and demonstrate true interest in working for them.

5. **Expand on Your Career Objective**
   If the job you are applying for does not match the career objective of your resume (or if your resume has no objective), use your cover letter to state your career objective and to expand upon it. Detail your qualifications to handle a new objective, referring to your resume for support.

6. **Offer Additional Information**
   If you are changing jobs or you have been out of the workforce for a lengthy period and are worried that an employer will detect this from your resume, use your cover letter to explain. You may want to explain why you are changing jobs or why there is a large gap in your employment history. However, do not direct the employer's attention to an issue if you do not have a reason that the employer will find acceptable. In the cover letter, you may bring to the employer's attention a plant closing or another reason for a job search that does not reflect poor workmanship on your part. Always use your better judgment and, if in doubt, leave it out.

7. **Thank an Employer for the Interview**
   A follow-up letter after an interview is also important. Many people underestimate the importance of sending a thank-you letter to an employer after an interview. This gesture demonstrates true interest on your part, and it allows you to add any information that you may have forgotten during the interview. Sometimes a small gesture of business etiquette such as a simple thank-you letter can affect how the employer perceives you.

hail Tchkheidze/Shutterstock.com

The entire focus of your cover letter should be on the benefits you will bring to the employer.

THE INSIDE SCOOP

"Thank you notes are still customary. However, nowadays, some people will prefer to receive a thank-you e-mail rather than a written note. It's good if they not only convey their appreciation for the interview but it's also important to me if they put something in the letter that they remember from the interview that demonstrates they were listening, too. Some type of follow up is always important. Even a phone call is ok, although I personally prefer an e-mail."

Geoff Green, VP of Talent Acquisition, Brown Shoe, Inc.

8. **Request an Interview**
   By sending a resume and cover letter you are **implying** you want an interview, but it is imperative that you state the obvious in your cover letter. Do not rely on the employer to take action. Never end a letter with "If you are interested," "Please call me," or any other phrase that expects the employer to take action. *You* want the job. *You* take the action. Tell the employer you will contact him or her in the near future to arrange an interview. Then do so and follow up.

THE COMPONENTS OF AN EFFECTIVE COVER LETTER

YOUR CONTACT INFORMATION

Use a letterhead with your name, address, phone number, and e-mail address. Matching the letterhead used in your resume is best.

INSIDE ADDRESS AND SALUTATION

The most important feature of the cover letter is the fact that it is *personalized* and sent directly to the person in charge of hiring. If you are uncertain who this is, call the company. Furthermore, check and double check the spelling of the name. No one likes to see his or her name misspelled, and it shows carelessness on the writer's part. Include the person's title, too. The name and title will be followed by the company name and address.

INTRODUCTION: EXPANDING ON YOUR CAREER OBJECTIVE

In your introduction, state the purpose of your letter. Identify the job you are seeking. Additionally, try to grab the reader's attention in the introduction. Do this by highlighting an impressive accomplishment, mentioning the name of your referral, or by making an interesting observation or compliment about the company with whom you are seeking employment.

Include any additional information, such as reasons for making a job change or why this specific company interests you.

HIGHLIGHT YOUR BACKGROUND

Discuss your past. Highlight skills and accomplishments that are important for the job at hand. Refer to your resume (so that the employer will read it, too).

TELL THE EMPLOYER WHAT YOU WILL CONTRIBUTE TO THE ORGANIZATION

Talk about your future. Explain how your background will benefit the employer. Interject your knowledge of the employer's accomplishments. Demonstrating that you did your homework can give you an edge over the competition.

ASK FOR AN INTERVIEW

Take the initiative and tell the employer that you will call him or her to discuss further the matter on hand; that is, to arrange an interview.

Stick to this format as much as possible. Occasionally, you may want to switch the order of components four and five. Sometimes, first emphasizing the contributions you will make if hired and then reinforcing this with a summary of your background and experience is best. Either way, remember to keep the employer in mind and stress your ability and willingness to contribute to the organization.

THREE TYPES OF COVER LETTERS

RESPONSE TO A WANT AD

When responding to a want ad, try to get the name of the person in charge of hiring and address your cover letter to him or her. If it is a blind ad, use a standard salutation of "Dear Sir/Madam."

The best format for answering a want ad is to match the requirements given in the ad with the skills you have listed in your resume. Show that your abilities correspond to the employer's needs. In many instances, this will replace components three and four.

Because a blind ad is impossible to follow up, you will have to end your letter cordially with a phrase such as "Looking forward to your response."

INVITED RESPONSE

Frequently, you will send your resume and cover letter to an employer you have spoken with on the phone—one who has requested you to send in the details of your work history and background. In this case, mention in your introduction: "Per our phone call . . ." or "As you requested . . ."

In your letter you may also want to reference something you spoke about on the phone and expand upon it. Other than that, this type of cover letter will follow the standard format without deviation.

REFERRAL'S LEAD

If a referral gives you a lead who is hard to reach on the phone (or someone you would prefer writing to rather than speaking with on the phone), begin your introduction by mentioning the referral's name. If your referral's opinion holds weight, mentioning him in your cover letter will give you a definite edge over the competition. Other than that, follow the preceding format.

> ## Rules for Writing an Effective Cover Letter
>
> 1. Use a good stock of paper—the same stock as your resume.
>
> 2. Use your letterhead. This projects a professional image, and if your letter is separated from your resume, the employer will have your contact information.
>
> 3. Keep your letter short—no longer than one page.
>
> 4. Date the letter.
>
> 5. Write to a specific person—preferably the one in charge of hiring.
>
> 6. Direct attention to your resume.

SAMPLE COVER LETTERS

LETTER #1: RESPONSE TO A WANT AD

This cover letter focuses on matching the requirements of the ad with the applicant's skills. The ad appears in the shaded box in the right-hand corner of the letter.

LETTER #2: INVITED COVER LETTER

This cover letter accompanies a resume that an employer has requested to see. This is usually after a phone conversation with a potential employer who has suggested that you send in your resume. Here the emphasis of the cover letter is on the benefits that you have to offer.

LETTER #3: REFERRAL'S LEAD

This is a cover letter sent on the suggestion of a referral, who is an acquaintance of the employer.

The letter's focus is on meeting the contact in person, either for an informational interview or to discuss a job opening.

SAMPLE THANK-YOU LETTERS

LETTER #1: AFTER AN INFORMATIONAL INTERVIEW

Sending thank-you letters to everyone who helps you in your job search, including friends or acquaintances that give you leads, is important. However, sending a thank-you letter to someone who has granted you an informational interview is crucial to your job search. (See Chapter 17, Networking.) This gesture can impress people enough that they work harder to find you more contacts or that they intervene on your behalf.

LETTER #2: AFTER A JOB INTERVIEW

When an employer expresses interest and takes time to give you a job interview, it is imperative that you send a follow-up thank-you letter. This common courtesy can sometimes be the factor that turns an employer's indecision in your favor. Sometimes, even after a rejection, if a thank-you letter is sent, the employer may consider the applicant for another job.

Example: Cover Letter #1

JUAN ORTEGA
1124 Bakery Avenue
Bakersville, NC 90000
(555) 998-0090

October 18, 2012

Teresa Micelli
Box 7344
Sunday Times
1123 N. Center Street
Bakersville, NC 11244

Ad: **Administrative Assistant**
To be a liaison with public & clients
5 years experience, 85 wpm
Microsoft Word
Attention: Teresa Micelli

Dear Ms. Micelli,

I read with great interest your ad for Administrative Assistant, which appeared in the *Sunday Times*, July 14th. I am very enthusiastic, because my background matches the qualifications you are seeking.

As you will note from my enclosed resume, I have more than five years experience in the field. I began as a secretary and worked my way up to an administrative position at Martel & Martel. I type 85 words per minute and am proficient in Microsoft Word and Pagemaker.

I have always been complimented on the quality of my work and was personally responsible for designing our successful company newsletter.

Although I enjoy my current position, I would prefer a more challenging job where I can combine my creative talents and interpersonal skills.

I look forward to meeting with you in person to demonstrate that, along with my credentials, I have the personality that makes for a successful team player.

Sincerely,

Juan Ortega

EXAMPLE: **COVER LETTER #2**

SUSAN CHEN   1212 OTTER DRIVE
                                                 SMITHTON, NY 90000
                                                 (555) 889-8789

November 3, 2012

Michelle Irani
Process Engineer
Sealico Steel & Metal
700 Sparrow Lane
Tiger Creek, AK 90000

Dear Ms. Irani,

I enjoyed speaking with you on the phone earlier this week regarding a position with Sealico. Your division sounds exciting and your commitment to "total quality" is very impressive—a conviction I share with you.

As you can see from my enclosed resume, I have 12 years experience in metallurgy. At Pershall, my contributions as Process Engineer cut production costs by 14 percent and increased productivity. You can find out more about my accomplishments in detail and read some of the excellent recommendations I have received by checking out my LinkedIn profile at www.linkedin.com/ susanchen.

I am optimistic that my knowledge and expertise in metallurgy, as well as my business experience in dealing with customers' needs and material selection, will be an asset to Sealico.

I look forward to meeting you personally and will follow up this letter with a call next week to arrange a meeting at your convenience. I welcome the opportunity to prove that I can make an effective contribution to Sealico.

Sincerely,

Susan Chen

EXAMPLE: COVER LETTER #3

DASHEL JOHNSON
1212 SUTTON LANE
FARTHINGTON, PA 90000
(555) 979-8777

March 16, 2013

Anthony Tommasi
Vice President of Sales
Lesser & Lesser, Inc.
900 West Corvina Parkway
Marshalltown, IN 90000

Dear Mr. Tommasi,

Doris Chen, an associate of mine at Goodman Shoes, suggested that I contact you. As you may be aware, Goodman is presently experiencing a significant downsizing. I, along with three other sales managers, will be discharged at the end of the month.

Doris tells me that you are always on the lookout for good salespeople. For the past five years, I have managed the children's shoe department at Goodman, and under my management, our department was responsible for more than 40% of total shoe sales. I was also instrumental in developing a training program for new sales clerks that not only cut their "break-in" period but increased their efficiency as well. I have enclosed my resume for your review.

Mr. Tommasi, while I realize you may not have a position open for me now, I would very much like to meet with you at your convenience. I have a few ideas I feel could benefit Lesser & Lesser which I am sure you will find useful. Additionally, I would greatly value any advice you can offer me concerning my job-hunting strategy.

I will call you next Thursday to see if we can arrange a convenient time to meet. Thank you for your assistance and I look forward to the opportunity of meeting with you personally.

Sincerely,

Dashel Johnson

EXAMPLE: **THANK-YOU LETTER #1**

DASHEL JOHNSON
1212 SUTTON LANE
FARTHINGTON, PA 90000
(555) 979-8777

April 3, 2012

Anthony Tommasi
Vice President of Sales
Lesser & Lesser, Inc.
900 West Corvina Parkway
Marshalltown, IN 90000

Dear Anthony,

I want to thank you for taking time from your busy schedule to meet with me last Tuesday. Your advice was quite helpful and, as a result, I am reworking my resume to include many of your suggestions. I will send you a copy next week.

I very much appreciate the leads you gave me and have already set up a meeting with Milton Becker for next Friday. Please keep me in mind if you hear of any other openings.

I wish you continued success and hope I will have the opportunity of meeting you again.

Sincerely,

Dashel Johnson

EXAMPLE: **THANK-YOU LETTER #2**

SUSAN CHEN 1212 OTTER DRIVE
SMITHTON, NY 90000
(555) 889-8789

June 23, 2013

Michelle Irani
Process Engineer
Sealico Steel & Metal
700 Sparrow Lane
Tiger Creek, AK 90000

Dear Michelle,

I want to express my sincere appreciation for the interview on June 18th. The opportunity to meet you and become acquainted firsthand with the fine work you and your team have been doing has strengthened my interest in working for Sealico.

I think your plan to implement a quality control checklist is excellent. I feel this is an area in which I can be of great assistance to you. I am confident that my experience in setting up such a program will add to Sealico's efficiency and save you money.

Sealico is a dynamic and growing organization, and I would love to be part of your team. I hope I am extended the opportunity to prove that I can make an effective contribution.

Sincerely,

Susan Chen

THE JOB APPLICATION AND SKILL TESTS

☑ Excellent
☐ Very good
☐ Good
☐ Average

Prepare to Succeed >>>

Today, increasing numbers of employers are relying on applications more heavily than resumes. While a resume only reveals the information that the job seeker chooses to disclose, applications usually require the job seeker to offer information he or she may have omitted from their resume. Many of these applications are available on the employer's website and are used as a screening process even before a resume is requested. An application may also be requested even after the employer has seen the resume or interviewed the candidate. Besides relying on applications, many employers are also using a battery of personality and skill tests to evaluate candidates.

In this chapter, you will prepare a master information sheet to be used in filling out applications. And while little can be done to prepare for personality and skill tests, you will be introduced to some of the more salient features of these tests to help you become better acquainted with them and help you prepare for success.

THE RESUME IS NO LONGER ENOUGH

As the competition for jobs increases and the proliferation of resumes reaches an all-time high, more employers are seeking other means to obtain controlled and detailed information lacking in traditional resumes. Higher costs in conducting interviews and job training require employers to be increasingly cautious in screening candidates. Most employers are spending more time and money on extensive background checks for potential employees. Employers are making a point of uncovering padded resumes and stretched truths about skills and background. Although personality testing has met with criticism for being biased and for being developed by companies that are not regulated, these tests are easy and inexpensive to administer, so they are becoming increasingly common. While you can opt out of taking a personality test, the employer can likewise opt out of interviewing or hiring you. Know that a poor performance on one test alone will not be enough to eliminate you, if you are a strong candidate.

SKILL TESTS ARE BECOMING MORE CRUCIAL

A resume only reveals the information that the job seeker chooses to disclose. On the other hand, applications usually require the job seeker to offer information he or she may have omitted from their resume. Additionally, more and more employers are requesting skill tests to judge which candidates are better suited for the job on hand. These detailed applications and skill tests are more comprehensive than a resume, allowing the employer to more accurately compare and evaluate candidates. Consequently, employers often rely *more* on your application and your skill tests than on your resume!

Although resumes and cover letters are still crucial job search documents, they are no longer the single, decisive tools that employers use to screen applicants. Often, employers depend upon a system of *triangulation*—using three sources to supply information about a candidate. An employer will combine the resume, the application, and a battery of tests, ranging from simple skill tests to complex personality tests (psychometric testing) to verify a job applicant's qualifications. This triangle of documents must merge effectively to ensure that the job seeker obtains an interview. Checking out references may also be added to the mix. In short, a resume is no longer enough, and today's job seeker must be prepared for more.

BACKGROUND CHECKS

More employers today are becoming suspicious of significant inaccuracies found on candidates' resumes. Many larger firms are hiring professional background-checking companies. Background-screening companies have grown from just a handful five years ago to over 700 companies today. Some companies screen over one million resumes a year. Some claim that as many as 14 percent of applicants lie about their education. Many employers will fire an employee if they discover falsehoods in his or her resume, because an employee who lies on a resume is likely to lie and cheat at work, too. Don't stretch the truth on your resume or color it with a few "little white lies." The employer may do a professional background check, and any padding or fibs may cost you the interview and job.

SKILLS TESTING AND APTITUDE TESTS

The rising costs of employee training and the increased percentage of turnover are causing employers to use tests in helping them predict if a candidate fits the job.

Skill tests can include everything from a mechanical aptitude test (for many technical jobs) to tests that check vocabulary, grammar, and simple math skills, specialized software competencies and, in some instances, simple accounting skills. More complex examinations test problem-solving skills, such as those found in case interviews. (See page 225.) Employers will not interview job seekers who score poorly. You cannot prepare for these tests, so the only advice is to remain calm and do your best work if confronted with this situation.

PERSONALITY TESTS

A test that assesses a candidate's ability to do the job based on his or her personality is trickier. *Psychometric tests* try to determine interpersonal skills, honesty, and work ethic. All candidates take the same tests; thus, employers can compare scores easily and choose candidates more accurately. If someone applying for a sales job scored low on "social outgoing skills" or "level of persuasiveness," that candidate might not be an ideal choice for that job.

These tests can also select or screen *in* a candidate, rather than screen one *out*. Sometimes, if a person has a low score for a particular job, but his or her score is considerably higher for another available job, he or she may be interviewed for a more appropriate job. Additionally, people whose resumes are weak and normally would be discarded may be offered the job because they received high scores on their skill and personality tests.

Besides testing for sociability, these tests score factors such as assertiveness, flexibility, risk taking, thoroughness, time management, organizational qualities, teamwork, leadership skills, honesty, and integrity. Questions may have you choose words that most and least describe you. You may be asked to talk about things you enjoy doing or how you would react in specific situations.

THE INSIDE SCOOP

Sample questions you may find on a personality test include:

1. Mark the viewpoint most like yours with a (+), and the viewpoint least like yours with a (−):
   a. Better to lose than to hurt someone.
   b. I'm usually not good at making small talk.
   c. I sometimes lose control of my workday.
   d. It's important to follow established protocol.

2. Below are groups of four words used to describe people. Circle the one in each group that best describes you:
   a. discriminating – persuasive – considerate – likeable
   b. impatient – imaginative – easygoing – thorough

3. Write *agree* or *disagree* next to the statements below:
   a. I dislike having to change my way of doing things.
   b. Regardless of the situation, I must say what's on my mind.

4. Select the next number in this series: 5 10 6 9 7
   a. 6   b. 3   c. 8   d. 12

5. Select which group does NOT belong:
   a. k l m h   b. r s t q   c. d e f c   d. v w x u

6. Red is to orange as blue is to :
   a. purple   b. green   c. brown   d. yellow

As you can see, you cannot prepare or study for these tests. The only advice is to answer truthfully and honestly. Remember—if you are eliminated due to poor results on a psychometric test, chances are that the job was not suitable to your unique talents anyway.

Rising numbers of padded resumes, as well as the high cost of training and keeping employees, have made employers more suspicious about trusting resumes alone. More than 30 percent of employers now use personality tests in hiring and the number is growing. Some of the more popular tests are:

1. *Minnesota Multiphasic Personality Inventory Test* (MMP)—used to detect proclivity toward substance abuse and psychopathology. This particular test is used by more than 60 percent of law enforcement agencies.

2. *California Psychological Inventory*—used to predict behavior and mainly a tool to "screen in" candidates to place the right person in the right job for them.

3. *Myers-Briggs Test*—used to measure leadership and teamwork skills. This test is especially popular among Fortune 100 companies who frequently interview candidates for high-power positions.

An employer may use a background check, a skill test, and even a psychometric test before giving you an interview. Tests have become sophisticated, and a candidate can rarely fool or second-guess these tests.

THE JOB APPLICATION

The job application is also gaining increased importance for two reasons. One, because applications are tailored directly for the job at hand, the questions are designed to supply the employer with the exact information he or she requires to screen applicants properly. A detailed application can help an employer determine which applicants have the required skills, training, and experience to perform the job. Second, because each applicant is answering the same questions, employers can better compare applicants to see which are best qualified and thus warrant the time spent on interviewing and training.

THE INSIDE SCOOP

"Our candidates take a series of tests consisting of five components. We test mainly for sales ability, math skills, and interaction with others. We do look for benchmarks within those tests. I understand that some of the answers can be open to interpretation and if someone scores pretty well overall, I may call them in and try to clear up some of the gray areas I may have."

Christopher Townsend, Assistant Vice President, Retail Sales Manager, Royal Banks of Missouri

"For a senior level position, our candidates go through a battery of critical assessment tests including the Myers-Briggs personality test, the Watson-Glaser for critical thinking, another for spatial reasoning—up to nine different tests."

Geoff Green, VP of Talent Acquisition, Brown Shoe, Inc.

Monkey Business Images/Shutterstock.com

Many pre-interview personality tests will be taken and scored on a computer. This allows employers to compare applicants easily.

ANSWER ACCURATELY AND HONESTLY

Completing these applications accurately and thoughtfully is imperative because they are an important screening tool. If possible, complete an application at home where you can take your time and think about your answers. If you must complete it in the employer's office, ask for two applications so that if you make a mistake you can fix it. Bringing a small pocket dictionary to check your spelling is smart.

Be sure you reread each question and that you answer each completely. Often, only small spaces are allotted and you must be succinct—brief yet exact—in completing these forms. As you did on your resume, use action verbs that emphasize your accomplishments.

Never leave an answer blank, as the employer may mistakenly think that you have not read the application carefully or that you have chosen not to answer a specific question. If the question does not apply to you, mark it N/A (not applicable).

Answering all questions *honestly* is imperative, as more employers are checking applicants' backgrounds. A signed job application is a legal document, and many employers keep them on file. Falsifying information may not only disqualify a candidate, but can often result in an employer terminating an employee at a later date if dishonesty is discovered. Sometimes, an employee can even be held liable for losses he or she has caused the employer due to giving dishonest information regarding his or her skill level and background. Follow the old adage, "Honesty is the best policy."

OMIT NEGATIVE INFORMATION

If asked why you left your last job, never write "Fired." Do not write anything negative on your application. Simply write "Job was terminated" or "Wanted to advance with more challenging career." Furthermore, never write disparaging remarks about a past employer or company. Employers do not want to hire people who slur others or who have a negative outlook. On an application, less is usually more.

EXPECT "INTERVIEW QUESTIONS" ON THE APPLICATION

Applications are becoming more and more comprehensive, with employers asking questions that were normally relegated to the interview. Finding an application that asks "Why do you want to work for our company?" is common. Even such questions as "How would you resolve a conflict with a coworker?" or "What are your long term goals?" now appear on some applications. Therefore, review some standard interview questions and know your answers before completing an application.

Many employers require applicants to complete their forms on a computer or even online. Even those written in pen may be scanned into a computer database. Like e-resumes, many of these applications will be electronically sorted and selected based upon keywords. Try to use action verbs and keywords whenever you can.

THE JOB APPLICATION MAY BE YOUR FIRST IMPRESSION

Today, your application may be the first document an employer reviews, so make a good first impression. Ensure that you have answered all questions and have included all critical information. Your application should be well written, with correct spelling and grammar, and most importantly, it should be neat. Sometimes simply a neat and well-written application will give you the edge. Additionally, bring a copy of your resume with you. Many employers will welcome an application with an attached resume and/or cover letter. A neat and well-written resume will attest to your professionalism and will strengthen your chances of receiving an interview.

PREPARE AN APPLICATION DATASHEET

The job application will require more detailed information than your resume (such as complete addresses and phone numbers of past employers, Social Security number, and so forth). Therefore, preparing an application datasheet to take with you when you apply for a job is crucial. When you are required to complete an application on the spot, you should not rely on your memory, which could fail you and force you to return another day to complete the application. Be prepared. Bring your application datasheet, resume, and pocket dictionary with you!

FOLLOW UP APPLICATIONS WITH A PHONE CALL OR LETTER

Treat the application like a resume and follow up with a phone call (and/or cover letter) a few days after submitting the application. Demonstrate that you are interested in the position and request an interview. When you receive an interview, bring a copy of your resume and job application (if possible) for reference.

Job Application Checklist

☐ Bring a copy of your "Application Datasheet."

☐ Bring a copy of your resume (and cover letter).

☐ Bring a pocket dictionary.

☐ Use a black ballpoint pen.

☐ Print neatly—in case the application is scanned into a computer, printing rather than using cursive lettering is imperative.

☐ Read every question carefully.

☐ Answer every question concisely.

☐ Use action verbs to describe your accomplishments.

☐ Use as many "keywords" as possible.

☐ Include all vital information.

☐ Mark all questions that do not apply with N/A.

☐ Answer all questions honestly.

☐ Reread the application and correct any mistakes.

☐ Date and sign the application—many employers will not accept unsigned applications.

☐ Attach a resume (and cover letter) when possible.

☐ Follow up with a phone call (or personalized cover letter) 1-3 days later to request an interview.

C H A P T E R 14 W O R K S H E E T

APPLICATION DATA SHEET

Many of these questions may not be asked on the application, but as mentioned, it is better to prepare for all situations.

PERSONAL INFORMATION

NAME (AS IT APPEARS ON ALL LEGAL DOCUMENTS) _____

Be careful. Some applications ask for "Last Name First"; some don't. Be sure to read the application carefully.

MAIDEN NAME _____

SOCIAL SECURITY NUMBER (SSN) _____

DRIVERS LISCENSE (STATE AND NUMBER) _____

BIRTHDATE _____

NUMBER OF DEPENDENTS _____

PERMANENT ADDRESS _____

_____

_____

PAST ADDRESS _____

_____

HOME PHONE _____

CELL PHONE _____

FAX NUMBER _____

E-MAIL ADDRESS _____

PAST CONVICTIONS / CRIMINAL RECORD

Nature of the offense, date and location of conviction, and the sentence or probation may also be requested.

Some jobs cannot be held by persons with a criminal record. It is very important to be honest as this information is usually checked. For some jobs a certificate from the local police department (including fingerprinting) may be required.

(continued)

CHAPTER 14 / WORKSHEET (CONTINUED)

APPLICATION DATA SHEET

JOB AT HAND

POSITION YOU ARE APPLYING FOR _____

Be specific and be realistic. Be sure the job you are applying for matches up with your skills and experience.

You may also be asked to list a second choice.

DATE YOU ARE AVAILABLE TO START _____

"Immediately" or "open" shows you are ready to start work now or at any future time. If you have to give your present employer notice, take that into consideration when answering.

HOURS YOU ARE AVAILABLE TO WORK _____

Mornings, Evenings, or Open (if you can work any shift).

SALARY REQUIREMENTS _____

You can request "standard rate." However, in this case it is best to be noncommittal and write "negotiable" or "open," which means you will negotiate with the employer if you are offered the job.

EMPLOYMENT HISTORY

Unlike your resume, which only requires the employers' city and state, most applications require each employer's complete address and phone number. Most also want the name of your past supervisor as well as permission to speak to him or her about your performance. Past salary history and specific reasons for leaving past employment may also be requested.

CURRENT EMPLOYER _____

JOB TITLE _____

COMPLETE ADDRESS OF EMPLOYER _____

_____

EMPLOYER'S PHONE NUMBER _____

NAME OF SUPERVISOR _____

DUTIES _____

_____

_____

Try to use action verbs and key words. Stress your accomplishments and benefits you provide to your employer.

DATES OF EMPLOYMENT _____

SALARY _____ (per year or per hour)

REASON FOR LEAVING _____

Try to find a positive reason—"sought more challenging position," "desire to advance," etc. If you were fired, simply write "position terminated." Try to eliminate any negative answers.

PAST EMPLOYER #2 _____

JOB TITLE _____

COMPLETE ADDRESS OF EMPLOYER _____

_____

EMPLOYER'S PHONE NUMBER _____

NAME OF SUPERVISOR _____

DUTIES _____

_____

_____

DATES OF EMPLOYMENT _____

SALARY _____ (per year or per hour)

REASON FOR LEAVING _____

PAST EMPLOYER #3 _____

JOB TITLE _____

COMPLETE ADDRESS OF EMPLOYER _____

_____

EMPLOYER'S PHONE NUMBER _____

NAME OF SUPERVISOR _____

DUTIES _____

_____

_____

DATES OF EMPLOYMENT _____

SALARY _____ (per year or per hour)

REASON FOR LEAVING _____

SKILLS AND CERTIFICATIONS

JOB SKILLS _____

COMPUTER SKILLS (programs with which you are proficient) _____

(continued)

CHAPTER 14 WORKSHEET (CONTINUED)

APPLICATION DATA SHEET

KEYBOARD SKILLS _____ (words per minute—wpm)

FOREIGN LANGUAGES _____

CERTIFICATIONS _____

EDUCATION

DEGREE EARNED _____

MAJOR _____

MINOR COURSES _____

UNIVERSITY / TECHNICAL SCHOOL _____

GRADE POINT AVERAGE _____

CLASS RANK _____

ACCOMPLISHMENTS / HONORS _____

_____

STUDENT ACTIVITIES AND ORGANIZATIONS _____

_____

VOLUNTEER WORK _____

_____

PROFESSOR / ADVISOR _____

PHONE NUMBER _____

REFERENCES

NAME _____

ADDRESS _____

_____

PHONE NUMBER _____

E-MAIL ADDRESS _____

RELATIONSHIP TO YOU _____

Such as former boss, professor, clergy, business acquaintance, and so on

YEARS YOU HAVE KNOWN REFERENCE _____

NAME 2 _____

ADDRESS _____

_____

PHONE NUMBER _____

E-MAIL ADDRESS _____

RELATIONSHIP TO YOU _____

YEARS YOU HAVE KNOWN REFERENCE _____

NAME 3 _____

ADDRESS _____

_____

PHONE NUMBER _____

E-MAIL ADDRESS _____

RELATIONSHIP TO YOU _____

YEARS YOU HAVE KNOWN REFERENCE _____

MISCELLANEOUS QUESTIONS

Many of these questions are similar to those asked during an interview. For more examples see page 232.

Why do you want to work for our company?

What contribution do you feel you can make to our company?

What is the most common misconception about you?

What are your long-term goals?

How would you attempt to resolve a dispute with a coworker?

FORMER MILITARY PERSONAL

Either in addition to past work history or in place of it, you will be asked questions regarding you military record. You may even be asked to bring your discharge papers.

ENTRY & DISCHARGE DATES _____

TYPE OF DISCHARGE _____

BRANCH _____

LAST RANK _____

SPECIAL TRAINING AND SKILLS _____

PART 3

THE INTERNET JOB SEARCH AND NETWORKING

Overview

You've prepared your resume and cover letter—now what? This section covers the next important step that follows: networking. This part focuses on the main feature of networking—namely how to make important contacts and transform them into job offers.

The reality today is that one cannot network effectively without the Internet. But the Internet has its limitations, too. Pam Dixon, Executive Director, World Privacy Forum explains: "Job searching online has benefits, but it also comes with potential privacy risks that most job seekers are unaware of. The best outcome of an online job search is to reap the most benefits from online job search tools, while being realistic about risks and working to reduce potential problems."

This section discusses how to harness the power of the Internet while at the same time staying clear of potential risks.

THE INTERNET AND YOUR JOB SEARCH

Prepare to Succeed »»

The role of the Internet is one facet of job search that has dramatically changed in the past decade. At its inception, it was mainly used for posting resumes on massive job search engines such as Monster. However, time has proven that these boards have limited success rates. Companies today prefer that candidates submit resumes to their own dedicated company websites. Another notable change has been the proliferation of social media websites. Sites such as LinkedIn have quickly evolved into highly effective Internet job search tools, and many recruiters and hiring managers scour these sites for potential candidates. While the Internet continues to be a powerful aid, the main areas of job search in which the Internet has proven valuable in today's market are:

- researching companies you may be interested in working for

- targeting employers and hiring managers

- posting resumes directly on company websites or sending resumes via e-mail

- creating social media pages to display your resume and recommendations

- uncovering job leads through LinkedIn, Craigslist, and online trade journals and newspapers

- networking, especially via social media websites, groups and forums

- gathering information about your job goal in order to help you write your resume and select the most effective keywords

In this chapter we will cover all these areas and show you how to take advantage of them to meet your specific goals. While this chapter will cover using social media to conduct a job search and post your resume or profile, using social media specifically to network will be covered later in Chapter 17 in detail.

One area of concern today is the reality of Internet fraud and scams that are becoming more prevalent. Author Pam Dixon, an expert on online job search, is now supervising a website (worldprivacyforum.org) to educate the public on job scams and frauds that have resulted from dishonest individuals accessing resume databases. Some of her tips on safely posting a resume online will be discussed at the end of this chapter.

THE ROLE OF THE INTERNET IN TODAY'S JOB MARKET

Not long ago, most people viewed the Internet suspiciously and were cautious about using this new tool for their job search. Later, it became the job hunter's panacea. Job openings could easily be posted and resumes could be sent out effortlessly. But the onslaught of resumes on the more popular job boards overwhelmed most employers

While the Internet has not proven to be the ultimate solution, it has emerged as an extremely vital component in today's job search process.

and produced a success rate as small as 5 percent. Furthermore, with so many employers posting job openings, the number of options for potential candidates became overwhelming. Too many resumes and too many choices made this overcrowded and overworked area of job search somewhat ineffectual. Even local newspaper want ads proved more effective than the so-called specialized Internet job boards. Today these job boards are all but obsolete.

The truth is, while the Internet is not the ultimate solution, it certainly has emerged as an integral part of the job search process, one which can and should be used to great success. Two areas in which the Internet has proven most effective are in accessing corporate websites and in participating in social media sites to post resumes, and recommendations and to create a network of contacts.

Advancements in Internet job searching have also placed the shoe on the other foot. Now employers themselves are using the Internet to uncover information on prospective candidates in both their professional and personal life. Unfavorable

SEARCH AND RESEARCH

A few online job boards are still considered important for job searchers to check out.

CareerBuilder.com is presently the largest online job site in the United States. It posts over one million job opportunities in every industry, field, and job type. More seasoned professionals may want to check out sologig.com, a division of Career Builder aimed at the seasoned professional. Some have found Craigslist.org helpful for both full and part time jobs. Those interested in non-profit sector jobs and internships may find idealist.org useful.

THE INSIDE SCOOP

"After we have chosen the candidates we are interested in, the first thing we do is check them out on Facebook and other places online. Since we are dealing with people who are going to be taking care of children and will be viewed as role models, we must be certain there is no objectionable information about them on Facebook or elsewhere. If there is, we will eliminate them on the spot. We also check Case.net to be sure they don't have a police record."

Stephanie Yaffee and Sharon Radell
President and Agency Consultant, TLC for Kids, St. Louis

postings on Facebook and other sites and blogs can ultimately result in candidates being eliminated. Be extra careful what you post online. Once it's there, it may be impossible to take back.

Because more and more employers and hiring managers scour the social media sites to uncover potential candidates, it has become imperative that every serious candidate maintain a professional Internet presence, such as a LinkedIn account. If an employer cannot find any additional information about you, he may go with another candidate who has an excellent Internet presence. A profile on LinkedIn will not only put you in the running, but it will also appear in a Google search, putting your profile in the forefront. But again, be sure your profile doesn't contain anything objectionable.

E-MAIL IS CRUCIAL IN TODAY'S JOB SEARCH

E-mail has remained the one area of job search in which the Internet continues to be indispensable. Having an e-mail address is crucial, as many employers will want to contact you via e-mail. As mentioned earlier, having a separate e-mail account dedicated to your job search is a good strategy. Additionally, be conservative in choosing an e-mail address name. A silly name, no matter how cute or clever, will detract from your professional image.

THE INSIDE SCOOP

"Thank you notes are still customary. However, nowadays, you don't necessarily have to write it by hand. An e-mail is fine."

Geoff Green
VP of Talent Acquisition, Brown Shoe, Inc.

E-mail is now the preferred method of many hiring managers for receiving post-interview thank-you notes and other business correspondence. Use it, but don't *overuse* it; don't become a pest. Too many unnecessary e-mails can be annoying for hiring managers. Be sure to check and double check spelling and grammar on all e-mail correspondence. Most e-mail programs have a spell check tool built in, so be sure to use it. Don't be in a hurry to click the send button before you are certain your correspondence says exactly what you intend.

TEN WAYS THE INTERNET CAN HELP IN YOUR JOB SEARCH

Regardless of the various options you pursue on the Internet, having a top-notch e-resume, replete with the most effective keywords, ready to upload electronically, is imperative. Your resume is still your key to success, even online. Below are some of the ways the Internet can assist you in your job search:

- **Accessing corporate-maintained websites**, which post jobs available at that particular company only. You can do a web search using the company's name or combining the name with the words "jobs" or "careers." For example, doing a search using "General Foods and jobs" will take you to the General Foods corporate website where you can access an area listed as "Careers." This link will not only give job listings but also tips on what the company is looking for and even what to expect at the interview. You can also cull keywords for your resume from the job postings listed.
- **Accessing want ads** from local online newspapers as well as Craigslist.org for local job listings.
- **Accessing White Pages and Yellow Pages online** to get names, addresses, and phone numbers of contacts and corporations in any geographical location.
- **Accessing specialized job boards** that cater to your specific career.
- **Researching online trade journals** and industry-related articles to uncover job leads and names of people you can submit your resume to directly.
- **Subscribing to professional blogs** that not only keep you up to date in your career but can also serve as a successful means of networking.
- **Networking**—uncovering the names and identities of people who can assist you in your job search by becoming a member of social media sites such as LinkedIn.
- **E-mail**—for quickly and efficiently sending out resumes, thank-you notes, and other job-related correspondence.
- **Accessing websites like YouTube to view instructional videos** that provide job search tips such as mock interviews, tips on using social media, and even resume writing tips. You can also use YouTube to post your own video resume which you can direct potential employers to view.
- **Mapquest and other map sites** can help you navigate to a job interview to be sure you get there on time.

CORPORATE WEBSITES

Posting resumes directly on a target company's dedicated website is more effective than posting on generic job boards. Previously, many corporations relied on the larger job boards to find candidates. However, this has changed for the better. Today, most large companies maintain their own websites. Most prefer that you post your resume directly on their website so that it automatically enters their corporate database. Today, even when you answer a job post on job boards such as CareerBuilder, many times

SEARCH AND RESEARCH

To get a more comprehensive and perhaps less biased overview of a company, you may want to log onto either PR Newswire (www.prnewswire.com) or Business Wire (www.businesswire.com). Here you can search for a company's news, including recent press releases. You will discover what is happening at your target company, and you can learn what new developments are occurring in your industry. Another helpful site is the Internet Public Library (www.ipl.org) which features newspapers and magazines for every state, complete with job listings and information about local companies.

these sites will directly link you to the companies' own website. There you may find that in addition to posting a resume, you will be required to fill out an application.

It is also important to visit a company's website in order to learn more about the company and decide if the environment and job description meet your career goals. One warning: What you read on a company's own website is controlled information—they are telling you only what they *want* you to know. To find a more unbiased view, you should investigate them further. Search for the company online and read newspaper and journal articles about them.

LOOK FOR BUZZWORDS USED ON CORPORATE WEBSITES

Corporate websites can be helpful in other ways as well. Take note of the buzzwords the company site uses and incorporate those same words as keywords into your resume and cover letter. Be sure to read their mission statement. This will describe where they are headed, and it will provide you with information you should include in your cover letter. If your cover letter can explain how you can help the company achieve its mission, you will already have one foot in the door.

Of course, the most important reason to check a company's website is to uncover job leads in your specific field. Usually, a business will post all jobs available in all departments. Unlike the larger job boards, the jobs posted on a corporate job board currently exist, and candidates who answer these ads will normally be considered quickly. If your skills and experience match the job description, posting a resume directly on a company website gives you a greater chance of getting an interview than posting on a larger, generic board does.

GATHER INFORMATION FOR YOUR INTERVIEW

If you are granted an interview, the research and information you glean from a company website can be enormously helpful in preparing. You can learn about the job and about the company's future. Knowing the background and outlook of the company is advantageous in an interview.

HOW TO FIND A SPECIFIC CORPORATE WEBSITE

Finding a specific company or list of companies that would be interested in your skills is a simple process. A few of the most common methods for tracking down target employers' websites follow.

- Search engine: Using a desired job title and/or keywords that describe your skills will produce many hits. This is perhaps the most effective means available.
- Yellow Pages: You can search through them either online or in print.

↪ Trade journals: You can search through them either online or in print.

↪ Want ads: You can find many newspapers online, and check the classifieds there.

Once you have found the name of a potential target company, you can use a search engine to find out if they maintain a home page or dedicated website. Once you find the website, navigating it usually involves clicking on options from a menu. This is perhaps the most effective way to uncover effective job leads.

Although accessing corporate websites is emerging as one of the more effective job search tools, remember that nothing replaces face-to-face personal contact. Ultimately, most jobs are filled by people who contact their friends and acquaintances to steer them toward a job opening. Nonetheless, approach the Internet as a single option in your job search. Do not rely exclusively on it, and never let it replace more sophisticated means of networking to uncover leads.

SPECIALIZED JOB BOARDS AND TRADE JOURNALS

Many professional associations maintain job boards dedicated to a specific job area, such as health care (www.healthcareerweb.com). These, too, can usually be found via search engines and trade journals. Numerous trade journals now appear online, many for free. Some local library websites also feature an electronic library area which contains many newspapers and journals online for free. A free health-career journal such as www.healthindustrynews.com can be an indispensable source for keeping up with the health profession, and can garner names of people and potential employers to utilize in your job search. Social media sites can offer a greater chance of getting your resume directly to the right person in the right place, even more so than a cold website job posting. Subscribing to industry e-mail newsletters and groups is also a good way to network and to learn about recent job trends and to stay in the know about your field.

SOCIAL MEDIA WEBSITES

Perhaps the most significant advance in Internet job search has been the proliferation of social media websites. With the advent of Facebook, which was created solely to keep college friends in touch, an entire industry of social media has arisen with the singular goal of helping people stay connected. These sites provide excellent opportunities to meet people in your industry regardless of geographic limits. But more importantly, all these contacts can afford you the opportunity to network with people who can assist you in your job search, if not offer you a job outright. While job searchers used to rely on newsgroups, forums, and mailing lists, many of these have become passé in the wake of the more effective social media sites, as most sites now offer their own collection of forums and groups which have become industry standard.

SEARCH AND RESEARCH

One specialized job board that is becoming very popular is www.simplyhired.com. The site works in conjunction with LinkedIn as well as independently. It has close to five million jobs listed and allows you to sort the jobs either via a keyword(s) search or by job category. You can also subscribe to updates which are sent via e-mail. It is a site worth checking into.

While Facebook is perhaps the most popular in social media, the most important one for job hunters is certainly LinkedIn. It is imperative that anyone conducting a job search join LinkedIn. Other sites such as Plaxo, MySpace, and Twitter are also being used by job hunters, but LinkedIn has emerged as the preferred site for professional job search and networking. While each site has its own particular bent, all are basically similar in their arrangement, and thus once you are familiar with one, you should have no trouble signing up on others. Because LinkedIn has proven the most effective, we will focus on it.

Remember, even if you use LinkedIn exclusively for your professional job search and Facebook for personal enjoyment, any employer who does a web search on you will most likely turn up your Facebook profile, too. That's why, during the duration of your job search, be sure *all* of your social media pages, each and every site you are a member on, are in order and that your privacy levels are set properly.

WHY LinkedIn IS IMPORTANT

LinkedIn is perhaps the most revolutionary change in Internet job search and is quickly becoming one of the most effective means of getting a job, beating out many of the more traditional job search methods of the past. LinkedIn operates the world's largest professional network on the Internet with more than 100 million members in over 200 countries and territories. Not only does it provide an opportunity to connect with influential people in your field, but it consolidates many of the major components of Internet job search into one website, making your job search much easier and more effective.

With LinkedIn you can:

→ Post your resume—or better yet, a detailed profile complete with headshot and audio and video.

→ Update your accomplishments and profile as often as you want—automatically informing your contacts about your updates, eliminating the need to send new resumes every time you make a change.

→ Show off your achievements, stressing your skills and accomplishments.

→ Direct employers to your dedicated website or blog.

→ Display a number of recommendations from experts in your field.

→ Connect and re-connect with acquaintances (such as college buddies and professors) who can help you build a solid network of leads.

→ Search for job postings in your field.

→ Gather information about companies where you are interested in working.

→ Join professional groups where, besides making important contacts, you can find mentors who will answer questions and help you in your job area.

→ Answer others' questions—affording you the opportunity to show off your expertise and impress a future employer with your proficiency.

→ See how other, successful people market themselves, picking up on keywords and other information that can help you structure a more effective profile and resume.

→ Maintain an important online presence which will appear whenever an employer searches for you online.

While face-to-face contact will always be the best method to find a job, LinkedIn may be the next best thing to help initiate long-term business relationships.

GETTING STARTED WITH LinkedIn—YOUR PROFILE

It is very easy to get started on LinkedIn. Go to www.linkedin.com where you will register a user name (your e-mail address) and chose a password for future access. A basic LinkedIn account is free, although premium accounts are offered for a fee. For most job searches a simple free account will do. The main advantage of a paid account is that it allows you to send unsolicited e-mail to potential contacts for free, whereas with a free account you will incur a charge for each "InMail" you send out unsolicited. More information about paid accounts can be found on the LinkedIn website on the "upgrade my account" selection on the bottom bar. As a matter of fact, most questions you may have about any of LinkedIn's features can easily be answered by accessing their various help menus. You can also access the LinkedIn learning center at www.learn.linkedin.com where you will find information and tutorials on how to use the site. You'll find a variety of video tutorials on YouTube as well.

The first thing you must do, once you have signed up, is set up your profile. The website itself will take you step by step through the process of setting up a complete profile under the "Edit Profile" tab on the home page. Your profile is like your resume—except you have a lot more flexibility. Everything in your resume should be in your profile and then some. If you are currently unemployed, you should indicate you are "open to opportunities." Unlike your resume, a headshot can be added to your profile and many prefer to see one. It is always easier to connect with a face than a mere name and title. Be sure, though, that you choose an *appropriate* photo.

Next you will compose a headline to appear under your name which indicates your job title or area of expertise. Many people opt for clever headlines such as "World's greatest problem solver" which may be okay if you are not looking for a job but are looking for clients or other marketing venues. However, job seekers should keep everything professional and not be cutesy. A good headline will not only give your job title but may add a phrase to describe you area of expertise. Instead of simply stating "accountant" you should be more specific; for example: "Senior accountant specializing in analyzing and researching hedge funds." Your headline is the first statement a contact will read about you, so be sure it makes a positive and professional impression. Next you will enter your general location and the industry in which you are working. This information is important for people seeking out contacts in a specific location and industry. Back on the main home page, you will fill out the rest of your profile.

Next you will add your present and past work experience, with job titles and company names. You should be as thorough as you can, listing your major responsibilities on each job. Your education should also be filled out with your degree, and, of utmost importance, the name of your alma mater. Old classmates and professors can be a great help in a job search and many times the best way a contact finds you is by searching your college or university on LinkedIn.

One of the places you can really shine on LinkedIn is in the "Summary" section where you can list your achievements in more detail than you can on a resume. You can even have a subsection entitled "Specialties" in which you can include keywords that an employer will pick up when doing a search for candidates. Any special skills or languages in which you are fluent should be noted as well. The idea is to be as thorough as possible while keeping it succinct.

POSTING RECOMMENDATIONS ON LinkedIn IS CRUCIAL

"Recommendations" is another section which you should take advantage of. Most employers will want to see that others have faith in your talents. LinkedIn offers a generic "Ask for a recommendation" tab which has you choose what you want to be recommended for, who you want to send the request to, and a generic standard request note. While it makes asking for a request easy, it may be a bit too impersonal which could offend the person you are sending it to. It is usually best to delete the generic note and compose your own. Find out what your contact is doing now and make your note personal. You should also tell the person what you are doing and what he or she is recommending you for. This will give him or her a framework for a recommendation and make it more effective. Try for three recommendations if possible. The best recommendations would be from your most recent job written by a manager or executive in the company. If you yourself were a manger, a glowing letter from one of the people you managed would also do you well. This is another area where LinkedIn has a definite advantage over the simple resume which includes no recommendations.

"Additional Information," such as awards and honors, groups, and associations can also be included. And you can add a link to a personal website or blog, but again be sure these sites are professional and do not contain anything offensive or potentially embarrassing.

PRIVACY ON LinkedIn—CONTROLLING WHO SEES WHAT

The last area of your profile is your "Contact Settings." When you edit this tab, you will check a series of boxes which allows you to control and limit the type of e-mail contacts you are interested in receiving. If you do not want your present employer to know that you are actively seeking a job, do NOT check "career opportunities," but be sure you check "expertise requests." Many job offers may reach you as "requests." However, if you are currently unemployed and need not worry about an employer discovering you looking to leave, then by all means you should check "career opportunities," as this is the most effective way to broadcast to others that you are open for job inquiries. The other two important settings that a job seeker must be sure to check are "job inquiries" and "requests to reconnect." Selecting only the areas that interest you helps avoid wasting time with unwanted e-mails, such as business ventures that you have no interest in.

After you have finished your profile, you will want to decide who can access which parts of your profile. Under the section "public profile," click edit and follow the instructions. You can either make your public profile visible to no one or you can chose which parts you want others to be able to access. There is also a tab to import your resume as well as create your profile in another language. Once you are happy with you profile (it need not be 100% finished) you are ready to go to the next step—using LinkedIn to find a job.

TIPS ON USING LinkedIn TO FIND A JOB

Networking

Once your profile is complete, you are ready to start looking for job leads. Making contacts is perhaps the most important step. You will want to add contacts from your e-mail address book, as well as search for past co-workers or acquaintances you can

SEARCH AND RESEARCH

"Resume Builder" (http://resume.linkedinlabs.com) is an option which enables you to turn your LinkedIn profile into a beautiful resume in seconds. No more messing around with multiple Word and PDF documents scattered all over the computer. Pick a resume template, customize the content, and print and share the result.

invite to join your contact list. Many of these contacts can either help you directly or introduce you to one of their contacts who can help you. Using LinkedIn to network will be covered in detail in Chapter 17.

Using the Job Search Engine

Select "Jobs" from the top bar. Here you can search for jobs that have been posted online. Use a general job title or a specific area. For example, "copywriter" is better than simply "writer" if what you want to do is write advertising copy. After selecting a job that interests you, you may be taken directly to a company website to apply or be asked to post your resume.

Join a Professional Group Or Groups

Here you will not only make contacts but learn information that may be crucial for your career and job search. You can access this option by selecting "Groups" from the top bar.

The best way to learn about LinkedIn in detail is to sign up and use it. By experimenting with the various tabs, as well as accessing the help pages, you will soon become an expert in using social media to make your job search easier and more effective. In Chapter 17 you will read two success stories about people who got their job by using LinkedIn.

OTHER SOCIAL MEDIA SITES—PLAXO, TWITTER, AND FACEBOOK

While most experts agree that LinkedIn is the most important social media website for job searches and professional networking, other major sites such as Plaxo and Twitter should not be overlooked. Plaxo boasts over 30 million members and many of them are not members of LinkedIn. Plaxo separates contacts into "family," "friends," and "business" allowing you to control which information is sent to whom. Twitter and Facebook can also be used effectively in conducting a job search. The bottom line is that there are many options for using the Internet and social media sites. You should never rely on just one option, but should "mix and match." The more social media sites and online connections you make, the closer you are to finding a job. Using a variety of sites and methods will increase your chances.

NEWSGROUPS AND MAILING LISTS

There are countless online newsgroups devoted to employment and job searching. Newsgroups are specialized bulletin boards for online discussion. Each newsgroup is devoted to a specific topic or area of interest, and visitors post and read messages. The groups are called *forums* and all the postings that regard one topic or question are

SEARCH AND RESEARCH

Most social media sites have similar structures: you create a profile, post information, and connect with colleagues and friends. More detailed instructions on using these sites can easily be obtained online. Besides the help pages offered on each individual site, one can find tutorials for these sites by doing a simple search. There are a variety of video tutorials on YouTube that demonstrate how to create an account and do a job search on a variety of social media sites.

called *threads*. Newsgroups are categorized either by specific industries, such as those that deal exclusively with jobs in computer programming, or by location.

Mailing lists can also help you uncover leads. Mailing lists (listservs) are basically discussion groups carried on via e-mail. Postings do not appear on a board but are e-mailed to each member individually. When you answer or post a message, every member on the list receives your message in his or her e-mail. Mailing lists perform the same networking function as newsgroups but are smaller and more personalized. You must first subscribe to become a member, and unlike newsgroups, many of the lists are not open to everyone. Many mailing lists keep archives of their postings. However, as mentioned above, newsgroups and mailing lists are quickly becoming passé being replaced by the social media websites which have proven the most effective means to connect with people in one's chosen profession.

ADDITIONAL USES OF THE INTERNET IN YOUR JOB SEARCH

A final important and often overlooked area of the Internet is its Yellow and White Pages. Use these to track down former classmates or friends who may help you in your job search. You may find connections on the Yellow and White Pages that did not turn up on Facebook or LinkedIn. You can also use the Yellow Pages to generate a list of local companies that may be interested in hiring. That list could also be used to drop off resumes in person to companies in your area that interest you.

Besides online methods for conducting a job search, do not forget the wealth of online information to help you in assessing your skills, as well as articles galore on effective job search protocol. Tips on everything from writing your resume and cover letter to job interview questions are online. You can also find out about current job trends and the constantly changing markets in your profession. Use the Internet, but do not have unrealistic expectations about the outcome. Finding a job is hard work and the Internet provides just one tool in your job search toolkit. However, if you integrate it with other more traditional job search methods, you will succeed.

PRIVACY ISSUES ON THE WEB

Before ending this chapter, you should be aware of privacy issues that have recently become a serious concern to online job searchers. When you post your resume on the web, many people besides bona fide employers may have access to this private information. To protect yourself, post only on sites that offer anonymous posting where your true identity is masked until a legitimate employer enquires. Never give your Social Security or your driver's license numbers over the Internet—even if a so-called employer contacts you and tells you that he or she needs it for a background check. Moreover, be wary of employment offers that involve working from home or transferring money—many of these are scams.

Be leery of phishing e-mails. These are phony e-mails falsely claiming to be from an established legitimate enterprise in an attempt to scam the user into surrendering private information that will be used for identity theft. Never give out your bank account or credit card numbers. Job offers that request you purchase expensive software packages for your new job are a definite red flag. Also, never give out your e-mail address book. Many companies steal these in order to send spam to everyone in your contact list.

THE INSIDE SCOOP

"Not every job is a real job. Be smart and research job offers. If it seems too good to be true, it may be. Take a hard look at quick, easy money job offers.

"When you do post your resume, use the privacy options the job site makes available to you. Know that scammers can and sometimes do get access to resumes posted in resume databases. If you have posted your full contact information, you may well get phishing e-mails, among other things. Almost all job sites now allow you to post your resume privately, obscuring some of your contact information. Use these tools; they can really save a lot of headaches later on, especially if there are any problems."

Pam Dixon
Executive Director, World Privacy Forum

SEARCH AND RESEARCH

To learn more about current Internet fraud and scams visit Pam Dixon's website at worldprivacyforum.org. Her website not only offers suggestions and articles on how to safely post your resume online, but is frequently updated to supply the timeliest information regarding privacy issues and job scams. Check it often.

CHAPTER 15 WORKSHEET

USING THE INTERNET IN YOUR JOB SEARCH

LIST OF WEBSITES TO CHECK OUT

JOB POSTINGS

_____

_____

_____

_____

NEWSGROUPS, MESSAGE-BOARDS

_____

_____

_____

_____

MAILING LISTS

_____

_____

_____

_____

COMPANY WEBSITES

_____

_____

_____

_____

(continued)

CHAPTER 15 WORKSHEET (CONTINUED)

USING THE INTERNET IN YOUR JOB SEARCH

TRADE JOURNALS ONLINE

_____

_____

_____

_____

SEARCH INDEXES/YELLOW AND WHITE PAGES

_____

_____

_____

_____

OTHERS

_____

_____

_____

_____

NOTES:

ELECTRONIC RESUMES, PORTFOLIOS, AND OTHER NEW RESUME FORMATS

Excellent
Very good
Good
Average

Prepare to Succeed >>>

Today as many as 75% of employers are utilizing searchable database programs to eliminate candidates and thus may be more interested in receiving an e-resume than the traditional hard copy. Because these resumes are submitted electronically, they require a unique format that can be easily transferred into a company's database of resumes. In this chapter you will learn how to rearrange and redesign your resume into an electronic format that can be easily e-mailed and uploaded to job boards. You'll find guidelines for selecting the most impressive and powerful keywords to add to your e-resume. Having the right keywords increases the chance that your resume will not be among those eliminated by a computer selection program or a hiring manager. You will also be introduced to other electronic job search documents such as the e-portfolio, and you will learn the best places online to display your resume to obtain the most effective results.

WHY YOU NEED AN ELECTRONIC RESUME

Today it is standard practice for most companies to use resume-tracking systems to scan incoming resumes and transfer the information into a database for easy retrieval. An electronic search that uses keywords and phrases to describe the perfect candidate can quickly select the most qualified applicants. Having a computer sort and select potential candidates is faster and cheaper than having a human do it. Resumes written and printed expressly for scanning are called "scannable resumes." They are basically identical to resumes formatted specifically to be sent via e-mail or to be posted directly to a computer database, referred to as electronic resumes or e-resumes. The proliferation of computer technology in selecting candidates has further intensified the need to have a resume that is "computer friendly," one that can be read accurately by a computer.

Today, even the most beautifully printed resumes sent by mail to an employer may never be seen by the hiring personnel. Instead, a secretary may feed your resume into a scanner, and an interested employer will view the unembellished electronic version.

SEND EACH EMPLOYER TWO VERSIONS OF YOUR RESUME

In addition to sending a high-quality formatted copy of your resume to an employer (and you should, because not *every* employer uses sophisticated resume-tracking programs), *you must also send an e-resume version*. It should be identified (preferably with an attached note) as the "scannable version," and formatted to be scanned easily and accurately. It must be

→ Formatted in ASCII. (ASCII is an acronym for American Standard Code for Information Interchange, and is simply a text-only file that contains no special formatting codes.) This version of your resume must not contain boldface, italic, underlining, fancy fonts, bullets, or anything that a scanning program finds difficult to read. You might compare it to the kind of document produced on an old typewriter.

→ On clean, white paper (the brighter the better), standard size (8 ½" x 11"), printed with a laser printer (or a top-of-the-line inkjet printer) in black ink, and sent unfolded (in a large envelope). The creases in a fold can cause letters to crack or fade, which will confuse scanning software. A complete list of formatting rules for e-resumes is found later in this chapter.

E-resumes on the Internet are handled in the same way. While most e-mail programs allow you to attach a document, an employer may not have the same word processing or publishing program you used to create your document. If an employer does not have the corresponding program, he or she will be unable to open your file. Today since most businesses use Microsoft Word, it has become the standard and attaching your resume as a Microsoft Word document will usually be acceptable. Many programs also allow you to convert a document into a PDF which will produce an exact replica of your embellished resume and can be read, for all practical purposes, by any computer. However, the fact remains that ASCII resumes are still the preferred format for Internet and e-mail uploading.

ADVANTAGES OF THE E-RESUME

E-resumes do offer advantages. First, they are cheaper. You do not need to spend money on fancy paper and printing fees. You will also save postage fees, because you will send your resume via e-mail or post it directly to job boards. Furthermore, most employers who maintain resume databases will store your resume for longer. Even if you are not hired right away, your resume will stay active and you may be hired later.

HOW TO STAND OUT IN ASCII

One dilemma exists. On one hand, competition today is fierce. With more people changing jobs and job databanks holding tens of thousands of resumes, standing out is critical. On the other hand, resumes have been reduced to bland, plain-text documents, where each one looks the same, making it difficult to stand out.

The solution is the content of your resume—what you say about your skills and accomplishments—and how you present yourself. This, rather than fancy formatting and paper, will distinguish you. In an interview, resume expert Peter Newfield stressed that today's resumes must be *more results driven than skills driven*. Your resume must stress employer benefits—how you saved your company money, how you increased revenue and profits, or even a list of your communication skills. Display the value that you will add to the company, and demonstrate what the company will gain by hiring you. (For more details on employer benefits, refer to Chapter 3.)

Nevertheless, even with a top-notch resume, you can still go unnoticed for one simple reason: the computer selects candidates based upon essential keywords that have been incorporated into the resume. If your resume does not contain the exact keywords the computer is searching for, it will not be selected. Unfortunately, a person with a mediocre resume who included the proper keywords has a better chance of being chosen than a person who is more qualified but neglected using the proper keywords. To compete, you must understand how to select keywords carefully and integrate them successfully into your resume.

Although the object is to make your resume computer friendly, never forget that eventually a person, usually the hiring manager, will read it. Never lose the "human touch." The task is to make your resume readable and convincing, yet computer friendly (that is, loaded with keywords).

KEYWORDS AND HOW TO CHOOSE THEM

The basic content of your e-resume should be the same as your formatted one; it should highlight your experience, education, skills, responsibilities, achievements, and most importantly, the benefits you offer the employer. The only significant difference in the content will be the addition of keywords in your e-resume.

Some believe that keywords should appear under their own major heading, labeled Keywords or Career Highlights. Others suggest integrating them into the Summary of Qualifications. These should immediately follow either your contact information or objective (if your objective is short).

Many logical reasons exist for this. First, placing all keywords in one section allows you to keep the rest of your resume the same, avoiding the awkwardness of adding additional keyword phrases throughout the entire resume. Furthermore, you will not have to change the action verbs into nouns. Action verbs read better, but computers most often search nouns. By placing keywords under their own heading, you ensure that the computer will not miss them while keeping the rest of your resume readable for a hiring manager. Additionally, highlighting keywords at the top of your resume allows a manager to scan your resume quickly and to see your qualifications immediately. Another factor is the search properties of some resume retrieval programs. Some programs record only the first 100 keywords, so having them up front rather than scattered throughout is best.

One caveat: do not overdo keywords. Your list should contain a maximum of 25 keywords or phrases. While employers may feed a program their own arbitrary choice of keywords, 25 keywords and phrases should adequately cover all possibilities.

Interjecting keywords into a resume requires a special skill and talent. However, here are some tips that can help you become proficient.

READ THE WANT ADS AND JOB POSTINGS ON THE INTERNET

What words does the employer use to advertise the job? In particular, note the industry buzzwords that are used. Compare the ad with others advertising similar positions. Words appearing in all these ads are critical keywords you should use.

LOG ON TO THE *OCCUPATIONAL OUTLOOK HANDBOOK* AT *BLS.GOV/OCO/HOME.HTM*

This handbook, produced by the Bureau of Labor Statistics, is an invaluable career reference guide. It lists almost every imaginable job and describes what skills are required. The job descriptions alone contain many crucial keywords. Many of the employers themselves use this guide when writing their ad to recruit new employees.

SCOUR TRADE JOURNALS AND NEWSPAPER ARTICLES IN YOUR FIELD

This will update you on current trends and buzzwords that are becoming popular in your industry.

CHECK OUT PROFILES AND RESUMES ON LINKEDIN

Look at how successful people in your field present themselves. Find them on LinkedIn and check out their profiles and their uploaded resumes. What keywords have they used? Better yet, check out a few profiles and see what **common** keywords are being used. Add those to your resume as well.

It cannot be overstressed: *keywords are crucial!* Taking the time and effort to create a master list of keywords for your e-resume is important. You may even want to prepare different sets of keywords to attach to different versions of your e-resume, each geared toward a different area of interest. Additionally, if you use a search engine to scour the Internet for job postings, you will again need your list of industry keywords. Take the time upfront to ensure that your list is accurate and complete.

PUTTING TOGETHER A MASTER LIST OF KEYWORDS

You should choose a sampling of keywords that corresponds to each section of your resume. For example, you will want a few keywords to correspond to your objective, specifically an exact job title and description. You will want a group of keywords that represent your Summary of Qualifications—how many years of experience you have and marketable personality traits. (See page 19 for a list.) Your experience's keywords should contain all job titles you have held, what skills you have used (see pages 17–18), and industry jargon and buzzwords that apply to your vocation. Key phrases like "increased profits," "reduced operating costs," and other short phrases that summarize your accomplishments without detailing them (see page 77) should represent your achievements. Save the details for the body of your resume. Mentioning the degree you received summarizes your education. Additionally, list certificates, awards, honors, and other pertinent information, such as proficiency in a language or computer programs. The worksheet at the end of this chapter will guide you in preparing a master keyword list.

CAUTION: *Be extra careful to check and double check the spelling of your keywords.* Remember that if a critical keyword is misspelled, the computer will not read it and your resume may not be selected, all because you transposed two letters or made some other careless spelling error.

Most keyword searches revolve around nouns and descriptive words that characterize your job. For example, if you instructed managers on the use of OCR programs, your main keyword would be the noun "instructor" rather than the verb "instructed." Another keyword from this example would be "OCR programs." Adjectives describing personality traits such as "accurate" and "efficient" are also important to list among your keywords. Of course, make sure that they are relevant to the job at hand.

AN EXAMPLE

The following ad appears in a local paper for an interior designer. It reads:

Great opportunity for a creative, results-oriented individual who enjoys a team environment. Position requires interior design degree, CAD knowledge, and 3–5 years of experience. We offer an exciting variety of project types, both commercial and hospitality.

In the area of objective, the keyword is simply the job title—Interior Designer. The ad emphasizes "creative" and "team environment," which in keyword jargon would translate into "creative" and "team player." Keywords related to experience would include the number of years of experience you have (assuming it matches the minimum three years required in this specific ad). You would also want to stress your expertise in CAD, and experience in commercial and hospitality design. These keywords are generated directly from the ad itself. Remember, only mention keywords if you can corroborate your experience in these areas and only if your resume supports them.

From the *Occupational Handbook*, you will find the keywords "prepare working drawings," "supervise assistants to carry out the designs," along with many others. This should give you an idea of how to find the keywords for your particular field.

FORMATTING YOUR E-RESUME

The second important difference in e-resumes involves their design and format. Resumes that will be scanned, sent via e-mail, or posted directly to an Internet job board must be designed for the computer. In other words, they must be computer friendly. This holds true for both scanable paper resumes sent to an employer and e-resumes posted directly on the computer. The rules are basically the same for each:

- *All e-resumes must be in ASCII (plain text).* Scanning programs and many e-mail programs do not perform well with formatted text, even in an .rtf format (a format read by most word processors). ASCII includes all letters, numbers, and signs on your computer keyboard. ASCII does not include:
  - bullets or other symbols not on the standard keyboard.
  - any advanced formatting capabilities. This means no bolding, underlining, italics, or even tabs. Indenting should be done with the space bar only.
  - graphics, borders, or shading.
- *Fonts must be simple.* Although true ASCII can support numerous fonts, scanners have a hard time reading many serif fonts and most decorative fonts. Use Courier, Times Roman, Arial, or Universe. These fonts are simple, clean, and easily read by scanners.
- *Fonts should be between 10 point and 14 point.* Do *not* vary font sizes for emphasis. Use only one font and one font size.
- *Length of lines should be limited to 65 characters.* This is the size of a line of text as it appears on a computer monitor. Lines should be broken by using the Return key (a hard line break) rather than relying on automatic word wrapping.
- *All text should be flush left (left justified), including your contact information.*
- *Lists should be indented 3 to 5 spaces, using only the space bar.*
- *The TAB key should not be used because it is not recognized correctly by ASCII.*
- *Margins should be at least one inch on all sides.*
- *The resume must be no longer than two pages, maximum.*
- *Your name should appear on the top of each additional page.*
- *No resume submitted for scanning should be folded or stapled.*
- *To improve the aesthetic look of your resume you can*
  - use all caps in place of boldface. Caps are read by ASCII and can be used to denote the resume headings such as OBJECTIVE and EXPERIENCE.
  - use asterisks (*) or plus signs (+) instead of bullets.
  - use hyphens (-) or double hyphens (--) to signify lists.

CREATING AN E-RESUME ON YOUR WORD PROCESSOR

You should make your formatted resume, replete with boldface, bullets, or underlining with fancy fonts, in an advanced word processor such as Microsoft Word. Then you can simply *convert that resume to ASCII*. Most word processors allow you to convert your document into an ASCII version by choosing that option in the save menu of the program. For example, in Word when you select File, then Save As, Word shows you a drop-down menu for Save As Type. This gives you an option to save your file as Text Only, which is a standard ASCII, computer-friendly document. If you must create an e-resume from scratch, you should use Notepad, WordPad (found in Window's Accessories), TextEdit (for Mac) or any other rudimentary word processor that reads and writes exclusively in ASCII.

Ensure your document is truly computer friendly after saving it (it will have a .txt extension), by e-mailing it to yourself and viewing it—just as an employer would see it. Alternatively, open it in Notepad and see how it looks. Did the line breaks and indenting convert properly? If not, you will have to do some editing in Notepad before saving your finished product. Remember to redo the fonts and font sizes so that they are uniform. You can easily do this by choosing Select All and then changing the font and size.

To see two example versions of the same resume, a fully-formatted one and its electronic counterpart, turn to pages 146 and 147.

E-MAILING YOUR ELECTRONIC RESUME

Sending your resume via e-mail or posting it directly to a job board is a simple task. Once you have your e-resume formatted in ASCII, be sure to save it to a file with a .txt extension. As mentioned earlier, a simple word-processing program like Notepad or

Sending your resume via e-mail or posting it directly to a job board is a simple task.

WordPad, which come with Windows, and TextEdit which comes installed on Macs, are perfect for e-resumes. Then follow the steps below.

1. Open your e-resume file in the appropriate program. For example, if your resume is called teacher_1.txt (teacher's resume, version one), and you have saved it in Notepad, open it in Notepad.

2. Select the entire text. Either highlight the entire resume, select Edit and then the Select All command, or press CTRL-A.

3. Copy the text by either selecting Copy in the Edit Menu, or press CTRL-C.

4. Open your e-mail program and insert your resume. Position your cursor at the point in your e-mail where you want to insert your resume, and either select Paste from the Edit Menu or press CTRL-V.

PDF FORMAT CAN ALSO BE ADVANTAGEOUS

Most employers today utilize Adobe Reader, and may prefer to see your resume in a PDF format. PDF stands for "portable document format" which saves a file in the exact format it was composed in and allows for any computer to display it in that format regardless of whether the original formatting program is installed on the computer. If you save your Microsoft Word document in PDF format, any computer, even one that doesn't have Word installed, will be able to view your resume in the same format it was created in. Many programs can now scan and search PDF files as well, and many employers may request them. The advantage is that you 'kill two birds with one stone.' The employer will be able to view your resume in all its adorned glory and a computer database will still be able to scan and deposit it in the repository of resumes. Having a PDF of your resume makes sense, especially today when many word processing and shareware programs offer the option of converting a file automatically to a PDF.

ELECTRONIC COVER LETTERS

Cover letters sent via e-mail or posted on job boards should be treated the same as an e-resume. They must adhere to computer-friendly ASCII formatting. However, cover letters you send by regular mail should be formatted. Most resume-tracking software is not used on cover letters; thus, cover letters are generally not scanned. Unfortunately, many experts believe that because these letters are not scanned, they are discarded rather than read. Many believe the cover letter will soon be extinct.

There are some who still believe that a well-crafted cover letter is crucial. Many employers do not use resume-tracking software, and many who do will read your letter anyway. Others will file your letter to be read later, if the computer selects you as a potential candidate. To be safe, send the best cover letter you can.

E-COVER LETTERS MUST BE CONCISE

A cover letter sent via e-mail must be short. Employers receive a lot of e-mails, particularly in response to a job opening, leaving them little time to read a lengthy letter. An e-cover letter *must* cut to the chase. It should not be an attachment, but rather should be pasted (in ASCII) into the body of your e-mail and should direct the employer's attention to your attached e-resume. In your e-cover letter you should:

↪ state the job for which you are applying.

↪ tell the employer where you heard about the opening. If someone the employer knows recommended you, be sure to mention that person's name.

↪ state that you possess all the required qualifications, which the employer will find documented in your enclosed resume.

Then *end it!* Skip a few lines, insert your e-resume into the body of the e-mail, and send it. If the employer has asked for your resume as an attachment, end your e-cover letter, attach your resume, and send them together.

Have a more detailed cover letter ready to send the employer if he or she shows any interest. You can mail this longer version later or send it via a second e-mail after the employer has contacted you. You may even want to send it as a follow-up after an interview. In this cover letter you should be more detailed and more specific. Its purpose is to demonstrate and emphasize your abilities as a "problem solver."

THE PROFESSIONAL PORTFOLIO—THE RESUME COMPANION

The professional portfolio is designed to be a *companion* to your resume. A portfolio is simply a collection of samples of one's work. Previously, only artists, models, and others in the creative arts used portfolios to showcase their talents. Artists would bring large attaché cases to their interviews containing samples of their paintings or graphic designs. Models and actors would carry an ensemble of photos to present their many poses and "faces." Quite recently the idea of a portfolio has reached almost every occupational field. Today's professionals find value in a portfolio containing their resume, letters of reference, samples of their work, records of their accomplishments, papers they have written or published, or any other documents that substantiate the benefits they have to offer an employer. While a resume lists skills, a portfolio demonstrates them in a concrete way. When skillfully planned and organized, the portfolio can be an invaluable instrument for getting a job.

Many colleges and trade schools are encouraging their students to assemble portfolios that exhibit a variety of the student's work, achievements, and recognition. Letters from instructors and student projects are important for an employer to see. For the graduating student who has little job experience, this can be crucial.

WHAT SHOULD YOUR PORTFOLIO CONTAIN?

Think of your portfolio as an expanded version of your resume. Just as with your resume, everything in your portfolio must relate to your objective. Do not add anything artsy, cute, or irrelevant to your career objective. Hobbies, clubs, and family photographs do not belong in your professional portfolio. Only material that supports your objective and resume belongs.

Your portfolio should mirror your resume. You list work experience in your resume; thus in your portfolio you should include documents or letters of recommendation that emphasize your experience. Try to document any concrete results for which you were personally responsible. Just as demonstrating your skills and accomplishments is the goal of your resume, your portfolio should do the same. Again, include items that demonstrate employer benefits. Just as your resume highlights certificates and awards, your portfolio can contain the actual documents and awards you have received. In short, anything that supports your career objective and demonstrates your ability should be in your portfolio.

HOW TO USE YOUR PORTFOLIO

There are several ways to use your portfolio, though you will use it primarily during an interview.

Checklist for a Professional Portfolio

- ☐ Resume
- ☐ Written samples of work (published articles, project outlines)
- ☐ Photos of projects
- ☐ Charts and graphs that demonstrate success
- ☐ Other materials that support your objective
- ☐ Licenses and certificates
- ☐ Awards (employers' or teachers' evaluation reports)
- ☐ Letters of praise from superiors or instructors
- ☐ Letters of recommendation

If you've earned an interview, the company is interested in knowing everything about you, and if your portfolio shines, it may help get you the job. You can also use it as a blueprint for a dedicated web page. Having your electronic portfolio on a CD allows you to send it by mail to a prospective manager. You can even indicate in your cover letter (or resume) "Portfolio available upon request." The idea is to have it readily available.

THE JOB SEARCH PORTFOLIO

Another type of portfolio is a more personal one. It is organized to help you, the job seeker, and is for your eyes only. It is basically a collection of job search materials, which you should always have available. Using a three-ring binder and appropriate dividers will best accomplish this. Inside you should have:

- ↪ all versions of your resume, numbered or coded to document which version was sent to which employer, on which date. Make a note in the calendar section when a follow-up call is due to that party.
- ↪ a record of each cover letter you sent.
- ↪ a copy or printout of every want ad or online job post that you answered.
- ↪ industry information, such as articles from trade journals, periodicals, or printouts from Internet sites, which will help prepare you for an interview.
- ↪ company research information from all sources.
- ↪ names, phone numbers, and addresses of people who you have contacted in the job search.
- ↪ a detailed journal of results from the job search—rejections, interviews, and follow-ups.
- ↪ a calendar with follow-up phone call and interview dates recorded.
- ↪ a "To Do" page, preferably at the beginning of the notebook, where you list on a daily basis what tasks must be done for the job search, and then check them off when they are accomplished.

Keeping a Job Portfolio or journal is imperative. You will send out many resumes and talk to many people, making it difficult to balance your priorities. Especially in today's electronic market, so many resumes are e-mailed and job posts answered that keeping an updated, detailed journal is vital.

In Chapter 19 you will find your Personal Job Journal. These pages can be removed from your workbook and placed in a binder. Make copies of any pages that you think you will fill and have them handy. These pages will form the foundation of your Job Search Portfolio.

If you prefer, use a personal-information-manager (PIM) computer program to store your information. Programs such as Outlook will allow you to keep a calendar and all your contact information in one place. Many free e-mail sites such as Yahoo! and Gmail offer calendars as well. If you have access to a scanner, you can scan all relevant newspaper and journal articles and keep them electronically for easy retrieval.

WEB RESUMES: YOUR PERSONAL WEB PAGE RESUME OR EXPANDED LinkedIn PROFILE

There are two ways to transform your resume into its own unique web page. The simplest way is to transfer the beautifully formatted version of your resume onto its own web page. Employers who receive your e-resume and want to see your formatted version can easily log onto your website for a look. Most word processors allow you to save a file in HTML (the web page standard), which means creating a web page dedicated to your formatted resume is as simple as saving your file in HTML and then uploading it to your web page. If you formatted your resume in Word or any other popular program, creating your web page will take only a few minutes.

If you are already creating a dedicated web page, take advantage of the available features. You can add graphics, sound, and links to your main page, transforming your web resume into a web *portfolio*. You can organize your web page exactly as you would your portfolio.

One link can take the reader to letters of recommendation; another link to research papers or projects that you can scan into the computer. You can link graphs, graphics, pictorials, and almost anything else from your page.

All of the above can also be easily accomplished with a social media web page such as LinkedIn or even Facebook. Everything in your resume can be explained in detail in your LinkedIn profile. Recommendations, samples of projects, even audio-video presentations can be presented with ease. You can get the same results as you would with a dedicated web page resume.

ADVANTAGES OF A WEB PAGE RESUME

Besides the advantage of creating a more aesthetically pleasing resume, one that uses graphics and other media forms to stand out, a web resume offers other benefits.

↪ You can password protect your site. Password protecting specific pages, or your entire site, allows you to control how much of your web resume various people can view.

↪ You can have a potential employer access your web page during an interview. An employer who has access to the web can open your portfolio during the interview, and you can conduct a tour that highlights your skills and accomplishments. Thus, you are actually using your website as a portfolio.

↪ You can interview with an employer on the phone. You can show an employer around your website as he or she talks to your from their office and views your web page on a monitor.

↪ You can download your web page onto a disk or CD and send it to an employer. You can do this either before or after the interview. The employer will have something to review even after you have left the interview. It also allows the employer to show your work to other colleagues who may be involved in the hiring process. Additionally, an employer downloading your web page portfolio to his or her computer is an inexpensive alternative to sending costly portfolios to each employer.

If you do maintain a website, or LinkedIn profile, you should indicate the URL directly in your contact information (on your letterhead) under your phone number and e-mail address, or you can even include a hyperlink in your e-mail signature. Thus, an interested employer can immediately access your website, allowing you to hold their attention. A well-executed website with striking visuals and graphics is another tool that helps you stand above the competition.

CREATING A DEDICATED RESUME WEBSITE

The actual creation of a website is beyond the scope of this book. One obviously has to have the proper software program and follow the instructions in the program's manual. Some web browsers offer "lite" software versions to create web pages. More elaborate programs can be purchased at any local software outlet. Additional programs containing libraries of graphics and clip art can also be purchased everywhere. The costs can run high. Many people with limited backgrounds in HTML have found it more cost effective to hire a college student to prepare their web resume. Remember, if you maintain a website that everyone can access, it had better look good!

MULTIMEDIA RESUMES

Another recent development in resume writing (which evolved from the website resume) is multimedia resumes. These can be resumes with video images, sound, graphics, or any other multimedia accouterments. They can be sent on discs as well. They can range from simple programs created with presentation software such as Microsoft PowerPoint to complex short video presentations.

Many tools are now available to an individual that only a few years ago were either unheard of or costly beyond reason. These techniques allow individuals to use their creativity in presenting themselves in a far more effective way than with a traditional resume. Integrating these new approaches with older, more traditional job search methods can generate outstanding results.

PERSONAL BLOGS

An alternate route that is gaining popularity today is the personal blog. Here you can present your unique views and personal observations.

Readers are free to leave comments and entire discussions can take place. Many people combine graphics and even video to enhance their blogs. A personal blog dedicated to viewpoints and information in your field may interest a potential employer. Reading your blog may create a desire for an employer to meet and interview you which can ultimately land you a great job. Again, it is wise to reiterate this caveat: Be careful what you post on the net. One who is looking for employment is not at liberty to engage in controversial subject matter. Limit your blog to viewpoints that will not anger or infuriate a future employer.

SUCCESS STORY

Sarah had just finished college with a degree in photography. She sent her resume out to numerous employers but was not having much success. She was worried that many employers wanted to hire photographers with more experience. While Sarah did have a good portfolio, employers showed no interest. Due to limited expenses it was impossible for her to send out color samples of her work with each and every resume. Sarah decided the next best thing would be to create a website that would feature her work. Sarah added a URL on her resume which was displayed prominently in her contact information. She also mentioned her website in every cover letter she sent, as well as mentioning it in every cold call she made to employers. In a matter of time, she was getting interviews with people who were now familiar with her work before meeting her. She set up a link on her Facebook and LinkedIn profiles featuring many of her professional photos as well. Using the Internet to her advantage paid off well.

WORKSHEET INSTRUCTIONS

This worksheet may be the most important one you will complete. Choosing the right keywords is *crucial* because without them, a computer will not select your resume regardless of your qualifications. Furthermore, keywords will become the focus in successful web engine searches when you scour the web for job opportunities. Therefore, take time now to generate a solid list of keywords.

Your keywords should represent each area of your resume. To help you select effective keywords, use the skill lists on pages 17–19, the action verbs on page 76, and the accomplishments on page 77. Remember that nouns and adjectives are more commonly used in search programs. Additionally, use the want ads and online job postings to find keywords and buzzwords that employers are using. You may want to access the *Occupational Outlook Handbook* as well.

First, select *all the keywords* that you believe apply to your objective. All keywords should support *one objective.* If you are seeking multiple jobs, make a *separate list for each objective.*

After you have created a master list, go through the list and circle the 25 best keywords. Include these in your e-resume.

CHAPTER 16 WORKSHEET

ELECTRONIC RESUMES

Resume Area: **Keywords:**

OBJECTIVE

(Job titles and technical skill areas)

_____ _____

_____ _____

_____ _____

QUALIFICATIONS

(Personality traits,
years of experience)

_____ _____

_____ _____

_____ _____

_____ _____

SKILLS

_____ _____

_____ _____

_____ _____

_____ _____

ACHIEVEMENTS (success words)

_____ _____

_____ _____

_____ _____

_____ _____

RESPONSIBILITES & TASKS

_____ _____

_____ _____

_____ _____

_____ _____

LICENSES & CERTIFICATES

_____ _____

_____ _____

_____ _____

_____ _____

(continued)

CHAPTER 16 WORKSHEET (CONTINUED)

ELECTRONIC RESUMES

Resume Area: **Keywords:**

COMPUTER SKILLS

EDUCATION

KEYWORDS FROM ADS

OCCUPATIONAL HANDBOOK
bls.gov/oco/home.htm

TRADE JOURNALS

BLUEMOND'S *WORD FINDER*

NETWORKING: UNCOVERING THE HIDDEN JOB MARKET

☑ Excellent
☐ Very good
☐ Good
☐ Average

Prepare to Succeed >>>

The most effective way of getting a job always has been and always will be by means of a personal introduction and recommendation from a friend or colleague to a hiring employer. An employer will rely more on a colleague's opinion than what he may read on a resume or application. Getting someone to go to bat for you and introduce you to someone who has the power to hire is perhaps the most effective means you can employ in your job search. The key is to find the right people and impress them enough with your talents so they will be happy to pass your name along. Sometimes, It's not *what* you know, but *who* you know.

In the past networking required a lot of time and effort, and you would have been limited to your geographic location too. Perhaps the greatest breakthrough in networking has been in the proliferation of social media websites. Sites such as LinkedIn and Plaxo have simplified the task of networking. Even with the help of the Internet, staying connected requires a lot of time and effort—there are no shortcuts. You should never rely exclusively on the Internet, either. It is important to keep in mind that nothing will ever replace face-to-face contact as being the most successful form of networking. As such, the Internet should be only one component, one tool, of your networking process and each should augment the other.

In this chapter you will learn how to develop a list of contacts, both on the Internet, with particular emphasis on LinkedIn, as well as cultivating face-to-face contacts. You will also find out how to utilize your contacts to get in touch directly with the people who ultimately have the power to hire you.

WHAT IS NETWORKING?

According to experts, more than 80 percent of all available jobs are *not* in want ads or web postings, nor are the numerous employment agencies aware of them. Some of these 'hidden jobs' may open due to company expansion, or employees that retire or change jobs; others exist because of the development of new products. How do you learn about and apply for these openings?

The answer is *networking*. Networking means seeking out personal contacts who can give you the names of potential employers, or better yet, put you directly in touch with them. Networking means contacting everyone you know who can give you referrals; friends, relatives, acquaintances, coworkers, professional organization members—anyone who can give you the names of people who are hiring.

While networking on the Internet is important, nothing will ever take the place of face to face contact as the most effective job search tool.

Remember, most people land their jobs from personal references, not from employment agencies or want ads. However, you must work at it. You must take initiative; control your own future. You cannot be passive and wait for an employment agency to call or a want ad to appear. Create your own opportunities.

Networking is a method of job searching in which you build up a body of support people (secondary contacts) who will ultimately put you in contact with potential employers (primary contacts). These primary contacts become your target market—the people you will send your resume to and contact for interviews.

Through networking, you discover which companies are hiring and which person (at each company) is in charge of the process. Your next step is to contact that person directly and ask for an interview. To obtain a job you must reach the person in charge of hiring and meet him or her. Networking will help you get there.

DEVELOPING A LIST OF CONTACTS

The first step in achieving your goal is to build a repertoire of primary contacts—names of people or organizations who are looking to hire someone with your skills and background.

Two methods for generating such a list are networking (asking people to assist you) and research (scouring websites, trade journals, newspapers, and Yellow Pages for leads). For researching leads, the Internet has certainly become the major source of networking. Using social media websites, such as LinkedIn, have proven to be a powerful tool for networking. Later in the chapter we will devote an entire section exclusively to networking via LinkedIn.

The first step in networking is to turn to the contacts you already have. Start by asking coworkers or other professionals in your field if they know who is looking to hire. College classmates, alumni, college placement offices, and bankers are also good sources to ask. Friends and relatives may also know people who can help you. Don't be shy—ask everyone for names of people that might make good connections. Sometimes a friend will give you the name of another friend who in turn will give you someone else to call. Keep calling and keep getting names of more contacts.

Always keep a list of who referred you to whom. When you call your contacts, mention the name of the person who referred you to them. Many times this personal connection will help break the ice and get you in the door, especially if the contact respects your referrer's judgment.

The best contacts are those who will personally intercede on your behalf and tell an employer about you. Although these contacts are uncommon, they can still help you build a solid list of names of primary contacts you can call yourself.

Call every name on your list. If the people you have been referred to cannot help you, ask them for the names of people they know who can. This is a numbers game— the more names you get, the better your chances of finding an employer who will hire you.

THE INFORMATIONAL INTERVIEW

One of the most effective networking techniques is the informational interview. Unlike a job interview, this is an interview you arrange with someone influential in your field; someone who can help you. The purpose of the interview is two-fold:

- You will get information and professional advice from an expert in the field.
- You will add an important contact to your network—one who may help you find a good job, or if a job opening becomes available at a later date will recommend you.

Is there someone in your field you have heard or read about who could help you? Contact them. Is there a business for which you would like to work? Contact the person who has the authority to hire you, even though you know that no jobs are presently open. *Make it clear to this person at the start that you are not asking for a job.* Explain that you are entering the field and the purpose of your call is to set up a short meeting (15 minutes) to get his or her professional advice. Most people will be flattered that you want their advice and will meet with you.

At the meeting, stress again that you are not asking for a job, but for advice. Ask for details about the job you would like to do. Determine what sort of experience is necessary. Learn what sort of problems come with the job and what is expected of an employee. Tell the contact about your background. Ask the person what he or she believes is the best job search strategy for someone in your position. At the end of the meeting thank the contact for his or her time.

Before you leave, ask your contact three key questions:

1. Ask if you can leave a copy of your resume—in case something opens. Some feel that a resume **should not** be offered at this point, since you made it clear to the person before the interview that you were not asking for a job. If you feel that offering your resume at this point may be awkward, you might want to send it later together with your thank-you note. Leaving a resume will have to be a judgment call on your part depending upon how well acquainted you feel you have become during this informal interview.

2. Ask if you can leave a few of your business cards (especially if you are not leaving a resume). Your business card should not only contain your contact information, but your LinkedIn URL and professional title. Some may opt to put a Summary of Qualifications on the backside of the card. It's a good idea to have your business cards handy and ready to distribute to anyone you meet who may be able to help you or pass your card along to someone else who will.

3. Ask if they know of anyone at another company who could use somebody with your background and qualifications. Calling someone at another company and using your new influential contact as a referral can open otherwise closed doors.

Immediately follow the meeting up with a thank-you note and resume if you hadn't left one at the interview. Then keep in touch with your contact. Call every six weeks to see if he or she has any news for you. You may also want to ask your contact if you can include them in your LinkedIn network. This way you will automatically be "in touch" with them at all times.

The informational interview is one of the most effective methods of networking. The interview will give you important information about the job you are seeking, as well as put you in direct contact with someone influential—someone who can intercede on your behalf, which is the best possible contact.

RESEARCH

Research is another method for procuring a list of primary contacts. Read the local business section in the newspaper to see which companies are expanding or opening new branches. Remember, every organization in your field (or one that uses people in your field) is a potential employer.

To find the names of organizations and potential employers in your industry use the following resources:

- Yellow Pages
- industry trade journals
- newspaper business section
- The Wall Street Journal
- Kiplinger's
- Money Magazine
- state and city directories
- Standard & Poor's (www.standardandpoors.com)
- Dun & Bradstreet (www.dnb.com)
- Internet search engines such as Google or Yahoo
- Social media search engines such as LinkedIn

Many states have directories listing all major corporations and organizations conducting business in that state. Most of these directories categorize the businesses by industry, making them a useful source for building a contact list. Always get both the name of the organization and the name and title of the person in charge of hiring. If you can only get the name of the organization, call it. Ask a secretary or an assistant for the name of the person in charge of the department that interests you. Get his or her name and write it down—but do not talk to that person yet. Because you will be calling that person without a referral, it is best to wait until you research the company. Be prepared with prevalent information before you make your initial contact.

WHAT ABOUT WANT ADS?

Do not make the want ads a priority. Most want ads generate so many resumes that yours can easily get lost in the shuffle. Some experts suggest looking in old newspapers and answering last month's want ads. If the ad is no longer running, the chances of new resumes coming in will be slim. If the job is still available, your chances for getting it are increased. With few resumes arriving, yours will get attention.

Be cautious of ads that don't give the hiring company's name. The want ad may be phony. An employment agency looking to increase its resume bank may have placed the ad. Alternatively, a company who has no job opening but wants to see who the competition is and check out who is in the marketplace may have placed it. A company may also have placed it as a legal formality, even though it already knows who it plans to hire. If there is no company name, be suspicious and avoid it. Begin with reputable companies that are hiring.

Perhaps the best use of the want ads is as a source for adding primary contacts to your network list. Call those companies directly and get the name of the person in charge of hiring. Contact *that* person, overstepping personnel. You may also want to search for employees from that company on LinkedIn or other social media and make a connection that way. All of these are better options than blindly answering a newspaper want ad.

This does not mean that you should never answer a want ad. Just don't consider them a number one priority. Use your best judgment. Always concentrate your effort on personal contacts.

TELEPHONE YOUR CONTACTS

Once you have a list of organizations and businesses needing people with your background and skills, set aside time each day to call. Call every one of these organizations! Find out if there are any openings available. If nothing is presently open, ask what future plans the company has. Get information. Additionally, get the name of the person who, if a job opening occurred, would be in charge of hiring. Write down his or her name and title for future reference. This is the person you will call in the future to ask about work or to set up an informational interview.

Do research. Learn everything you can about the companies that interest you. Develop a strategy. What could you do for them if you were hired?

When you have a clear idea of how you could contribute to a company, it is time to call the person in charge of the department that interests you. Tell them about yourself and give them an idea (do not tell them everything) of what you believe you could do for them. Ask them for an interview, or if you can at least send them your resume. If you can impress the employers enough, or arouse their curiosity, you may just get an interview (and a job) even though nothing is presently open.

KEEP A JOURNAL

Always keep an updated journal. Record each employer who expresses an interest in you on your master list. This is your target market. In your journal, record all of your activities. Note if you send an employer a resume or other correspondence. Do the same for all phone calls and meetings. Record the date and the outcome of each, and always follow up.

As you'll see in Chapter 19, the journal can be part of your job search portfolio or in a computer personal information manager (PIM) program, such as Outlook. You may want to ask your face-to-face contacts if they mind if you add them to your LinkedIn network. If they don't mind and you add them, they will already be set up in your computerized journal.

FOLLOW UP

Give your contact approximately one week to receive your resume or cover letter and to review it. Then follow up. Call and ask if he or she received your resume. Tell them that you are looking forward to meeting in person at a possible interview. Be polite, but be firm. If he or she tells you that the position has been filled or that you will not be interviewed, ask your favorite question: Do you know anyone else who would be interested in someone with my background?

Even if a job is not presently available, call your target employers every month to check on the situation. Make sure they still remember you. Thus, if a job opens, hopefully your name will come to mind.

Keep adding to your contacts and always follow up. Persistence is crucial. Thomas Edison famously said, "Genius is 1 percent inspiration and 99 percent perspiration."

USING LinkedIn TO NETWORK

Social media sites such as LinkedIn were created for the sole purpose of networking and getting people connected. Roughly one million new members join LinkedIn every week, a rate equivalent to more than one new member per second. It is understandable that having so many potential contacts at your fingertips can be a great help in one's job search.

Before adding contacts to your network, it is imperative that your profile is as thorough as it can be. Think of your profile as your "home base"; you want to fix it up and make it impressive before you invite guests in. Once your profile is finished, it will do little good if you leave it idle without inviting others to see it.

How do you build or grow a network, and which contacts should you target? There are two trends of thought regarding amassing contacts. Some feel the more the merrier and that one should strive for numbers, shooting for adding as many contacts as possible. There are problems with this approach. First of all, to network successfully one has to be in touch with his or her major contacts constantly to keep them up to date and in their minds. Having too many contacts, many of whom will not be able or willing to help, can make this task almost impossible. Also, in job search, quality is more important that quantity. Having a handful of the right people and most influential people in your network can produce better results than having hundreds of contacts that ultimately are of little use. Also, when an employer sees that you have hundreds of contacts, it may appear you are not selective and are willing to connect with anyone, giving the employer a bad impression.

The second and perhaps more effective method is to build a solid network of contacts that can and will be instrumental in helping you in your search. Like your face-to-face contact list, the most valuable contacts are the people you already know. Since most of these people are probably already in your e-mail address book, you can easily add them to your LinkedIn network. LinkedIn can import your list directly from most major e-mail providers. Select the "contacts" tab on the top "LinkedIn" bar and choose "add connections." From there you will be taken to a screen which will prompt you for your e-mail address. LinkedIn will then import you entire e-mail address book. The next screen will display those contacts who are already members of LinkedIn. From that list, you will select only those members you want to add to your personal LinkedIn network. Afterwards, LinkedIn will display a list of the remaining contacts from your address book that are not members of LinkedIn. You can choose to send them an invitation to join, if you would also like them in your network. It is best to select only those contacts that are professionals or have the ability to get you in touch with people in your profession.

There are probably many people that you know who could help you that are not in your e-mail address book, such as old classmates, professors, past co-workers and colleagues who are already members of LinkedIn. LinkedIn makes it easy to find these contacts and invite them to join your network. After selecting the "add connections" link you will find a top bar with tabs. One tab is entitled "colleagues" and another "classmates." Each tab will take you to a screen where you will enter a past company you worked for and the years of employment there. A search will then bring up any of LinkedIn's hundred million plus members that also worked at that company during that time. Again, select from the list of those names the contacts you want to invite to your network. The same thing is true for classmates. You enter your alma mater, the years you attended and area of study and a list of LinkedIn members that match your criteria will appear for you to choose from. "People who you may know" will take you to a list of contacts who are not in your network but are part of your contacts network. Chances are you know many of these people and may feel you should add some of them to your network as well. All of these contacts you've added so far are either people you know personally or have some sort of personal connection to. If there are specific people you have met that you want to add, you can do a search for them under "people" in the top bar on the right. You can access the advanced search option where you can add additional information to help identify the person you are looking for as well as limit the search to the right person. You would be surprised how many LinkedIn members share the same name.

Connections on LinkedIn are categorized in a hierarchical format. People who have joined your network that you know personally are your "First-degree connections." They are part of your network and you can access them directly through LinkedIn. "Second-degree members" are people who know at least one person in your network. You can only contact them through a first-degree member. In this case you would ask your friend who is already in your network to introduce you to his or her friend. "Third-degree members" are people who know at least one of your second-degree connections. You will have to go through a first- and second-degree connection to enlist them. When you click on "network statistics" in the contacts tab, LinkedIn will show you how many first-, second- and third-degree connections you have—and how many people you have the ability to connect with just from your network alone.

In many instances you will want to add contacts outside of your acquaintances such as influential people in your field whom you have no prior connection to. This would include hiring managers, employees of a company you would like to work for, and industry people who are respected. Here you will need to do some research, but LinkedIn helps simplify that job as well. You can search companies (and people) via names and keywords. This option is found on the top bar at the upper right hand side of the screen. Clicking on "people" will reveal that you can choose to search for companies and jobs too. If you are looking for the hiring manager of a specific company, you can enter that in the search bar or press the advanced option which will allow you to limit your search by adding specific locations, industries, keywords, etc. Of course, chances are that neither you nor your contacts will know these people and you will have to either find someone to join your network who does know them and is willing to make the connection for you or send them an invitation via an unsolicited e-mail, called an InMail. That party's e-mail address will only be given to you if they decide to accept your InMail.

USING LinkedIn GROUPS TO NETWORK

Another way to network on LinkedIn is to join LinkedIn groups. Currently there are over 650,000 groups on LinkedIn, with the largest amassing 200,000 members. A member can join up to 50 groups. To find appropriate groups to join, click on the "groups" option from the main LinkedIn home bar and select "groups directory." You can search for a group by industry or keywords, which will generate a large number of groups from which you will select those you feel most appropriate for your specific job-related interests. Most groups require that you be accepted before you can access the group and post information. Once you are accepted you are free to start a discussion, join

SUCCESS STORY

Here are a few stories that illustrate successes two different people had with LinkedIn. Notice how each one used the website in a different way, each to his or her own advantage.

JOEL G. USES LINKEDIN AS AN ALTERNETE ROUTE

Joel G. noticed a job posting online which requested that a resume be posted on the company website and an application filled out. Instead of following this option, Joel chose another route. He did a search on LinkedIn and uncovered the names of five employees who worked for that particular company and had LinkedIn accounts. Joel chose the one with whom he felt he held many common interests and sent him an InMail, which the employee accepted. After Joel connected with him, he asked him about the company in general and in particular about the job opening he was interested in. The employee was friends with the hiring manager and forwarded Joel's resume with his recommendation to him. Joel was called in for an interview and got the job.

MARY R. CONNECTS WITH A PAST CLASSMATE VIA LINKEDIN

Mary R. left the workforce to raise her two daughters. Now that her girls were in school, she wanted to return to work. It had been seven years since her last job, marketing for a women's wear company, and she was having trouble getting interviews. She signed onto LinkedIn and did a search for classmates that had graduated from her alma mater the same year she did. A classmate she remembered, Deborah M., was also working in women's wear and Mary connected with her. She did not ask for a job at first but exchanged e-mails on topics involving fashion and working in the field. Through Deborah, she was able to connect with others in her job market and even joined a marketing group, enabling her to build an even larger network. By taking part in group discussions, Mary soon developed a reputation for her wit and her incisive comments. From her participation, she was able to solicit three solid recommendations, including an outstanding one from her friend Deborah, all of which were posted to her profile. After becoming more familiar with the people in her network, she let everyone know she was looking for employment by simply updating her profile (which saved her the task of sending out dozens of emails). Mary's networking led to two solid job offers.

SEARCH AND RESEARCH

LinkedIn provides a tutorial site at *learn.linkedin.com*. It is an online user's guide where you can master all of the different features you'll find on LinkedIn. From a brief overview to very detailed tips, you'll find all of these in this section. Instructional videos can also be found here, as well as on YouTube. You can use the tutorial to get tips on everything from creating your profile to growing your network and using LinkedIn groups. You can also access "new on LinkedIn" to keep up to date on new features that are being added all the time. Important developments in how you can use LinkedIn are found on the blog, which is also accessed through *learn.linkedin.com*. You can check the blog's archives by subject matter. For example, if you check out "students" you will find a variety of articles that explain how a student can best use LinkedIn to find a job. Frequently checking out the "learn LinkedIn" website can prove very useful in harnessing the power of the Internet in your job search.

---

one, or follow one. You can also access a list of members from the "members" tab and see how closely you are connected to them (first, second or third degree) and send a message to them as well. Joining relevant LinkedIn groups can help you:

↪ gather information on your career

↪ find out the latest developments in your industry

↪ discover who the "movers and shakers" are

↪ show off your expertise and impress possible future employers

↪ develop relationships with people in your industry who may later be willing to join your network and help you in your job search

↪ learn about job postings which have been posted on the group for its members

One caveat here: Beware of spammers. Spammers can infiltrate a group and if you are not careful, you can find yourself inundated with spam and fraudulent offers. Be selective and be leery of messages that seem risky.

USING OTHER SOCIAL MEDIA SITES TO NETWORK

Even with the growing number of members on LinkedIn, you probably have many friends and acquaintances that could help you in your job search that are not yet on LinkedIn. Many of them may be members of Facebook, Twitter, Plaxo, or other popular social media sites. That's why you should not limit your internet networking to LinkedIn alone. Scour other sites to find more contacts. Most of these sites fundamentally work in the same way as LinkedIn, and offer "help pages" to guide one through the sign up as well as explain the particular features they provide. Once you have found contacts on other sites, you might want to invite them to join you on LinkedIn, so your main job search contacts will all be under one roof.

CHAPTER 17 / CHECKLIST

Networking is an important, if not the most important, component in your job search. Using many different avenues to network is best. While you should aim for face-to-face contact, social media websites such as LinkedIn and Plaxo have become successful means of networking. You should certainly use a variety of networking tactics. The more nets you cast, the greater your chances of capturing the job you want.

The worksheets for keeping track of your networking contacts can be found in Chapter 19: Personal Job Journal. The journal will help you generate a list of contacts, secondary and primary, and will also help you keep track of them all during your job search.

Overview

No matter how excellent your resume is, and how effective your networking, in the end, if you do not shine during your interview, you may be eliminated right before your reach the finish line. Everything in your job search leads to this final evaluation, so you must be prepared to outdo the competition one last time. This final part of the workbook will focus on the interview—how to prepare for it, what to expect, how to deal with difficult or awkward questions, and how to handle yourself and present a professional image. The interview is no place to be shy and reticent; you have to be confident and speak up.

Geoff Green, Vice President of Talent Acquisition at Brown Shoe, Inc., interviews as many as four hundred candidates a year and has the following advice:

"If someone is applying for a job in sales, I take careful note of how they conduct themselves during the interview. A person in sales should be used to presenting and I expect them to be particularly articulate during the interview. Most importantly, are they able to 'close the sale?' At the end of the interview, are they able to say, 'Are there any objections you may have to my candidacy?' or add anything else to close the sale. After all, closing a sale is what they plan to do for our company. For me, the end of the interview is the most important part especially if I am interviewing someone for a sales position."

In Chapter 19 you will find a job journal. While many computer and web-based e-mail programs supply calendars and address books, it is always good to keep a hard copy handy. Also, the journal in this workbook allows you to keep a highly detailed digest of your job search endeavors. This will not only keep you on track but will help you strategize and plan your future job search activities.

THE JOB INTERVIEW

☑ Excellent
☐ Very good
☐ Good
☐ Average

Prepare to Succeed ≫

In this chapter you will learn how to prepare for an interview and what to expect during the interview. You will be introduced to a variety of interview techniques that have become ubiquitous in today's job market and you will become familiar with the questions you will most likely encounter during the interview. Although there is not always a "right answer," you will discover the type of answers employers are looking for. You will also learn what questions **you** should ask the employer during the interview, as well as what you should wear and how to conduct yourself during and after the interview. Remember, the singular goal of the resume and all your job search efforts is to get you an interview. Ultimately it is the interview that will get you the job. It is therefore crucial that you master this chapter and its techniques in order to ace your interview and make the type of impression that will result in your landing the job you most desire.

PRE-INTERVIEW PREPARATION

THE INTERVIEW GETS YOU THE JOB

The interview is the most important component of the job search process. While your resume and cover letter get you the interview, the interview, and how well you perform during it, ultimately gets you the job. Usually, numerous candidates are interviewed and how well you outperform the competition will determine the final outcome. How you present yourself and the image you project will be crucial factors in getting the job you want.

Although your skills and accomplishments are documented in your resume, these alone are usually insufficient. How you interact with your employer and coworkers may prove more important to a hiring manager than your skill level. A major objective of the interview is to unmask your true personality and to demonstrate your ability to work with others. While you cannot control the chemistry between you and the interviewer, one thing is true: the more you prepare for the interview, the more you will impress the employer and increase your chances of being hired.

YOU *CAN* CREATE CHEMISTRY

Researching the company and job is vital. If you understand the skills employers are looking for and the image they expect from their employees, you can create that all-important chemistry.

Employers want to believe that your primary motive for seeking work with them is not just the paycheck. They want to be convinced that the company's reputation excites you and makes you want to work there. If you can convey such enthusiasm, chemistry will follow.

RESEARCHING THE COMPANY, THE JOB, AND THE EMPLOYER IS YOUR KEY TO CREATING A FAVORABLE IMPRESSION, A PROFESSIONAL IMAGE, AND ULTIMATELY, GOOD CHEMISTRY BETWEEN YOU AND THE EMPLOYER.

WHAT AN EMPLOYER LOOKS FOR

An employer will consider two basic questions. First, do you have the skills and experience required for the job? Second, are you the type of person the company wants to employ? To decide the latter, the employer looks for two qualities. First, your ethics—are you honest, reliable, and dependable? Are you the type that will frequently call in sick and leave after two months? Will you integrate well with your fellow workers, get along with the employer, and be enthusiastic about the company and your job?

The employer uses the interview to get an overall picture of you in order to gauge how well you will fit into the company. Most interview questions will focus on the following issues.

Substantiate Your Resume

You claim you have the skills required—now prove it! The interviewer will probe and ask questions to verify that your resume is not exaggerated or inflated. You may be asked detailed technical questions or how you would handle a specific problem that might be part of your job. You will be asked to expand on statements in your resume and to give concrete examples. You may even be given a written skill test during the interview or prior to it. Additionally, many employers may opt for a *cast interview* (discussed later in this chapter) to see how well you use your skills to solve speculative problems that you may encounter on the job. An interviewer may also raise questions about your education. Be prepared to talk about what you wrote in your resume and to furnish details, as well as to demonstrate your problem-solving skills on the spot.

THE INSIDE SCOOP

"The resume is crucial in our interview process. We use it as a basis to ask questions regarding past work experience. One of the main goals in our interview is to uncover any large gaps in an applicant's work history. If they can explain those gaps sufficiently, they will still be in the running."

Stephanie Yaffee and Sharon Radell
President and Agency Consultant
TLC for Kids, St. Louis, Missouri

If you have obvious gaps in your work history, you can be sure this will also be brought up during the interview. Be sure you can explain those gaps satisfactorily.

"Check Out" Your Personality

You will be asked questions about past employers—how well you got along with them, why you left your last job, and how you handle stress. You may be asked how you think your last employer will talk about you and how many days you were absent during the past year. The object is to determine that you are hardworking, ethical, and able to work well with others. Again, psychometric tests may be given to determine if your personality is a fit for the job at hand. Therefore, do your research and be prepared.

Assess Your Value and Determine Your Salary

The employer wants to know that your contributions to the organization will be greater than the cost of hiring you. Although you should never bring up the question of salary (especially on a first interview), be prepared to negotiate if the employer brings up the issue. Know the accepted salary range for your position before going into the interview. Clarify benefits, vacation time, and working conditions, if the issues are raised. Unfortunately, accepting a lower salary is sometimes a major factor in getting the job. Decide on the lowest salary you will accept if the job is offered on the spot, but always try to negotiate higher or for more benefits.

HOW TO SELL YOURSELF

Everything you do during the interview will be noticed. Not only what you say, but how you say it. If you fidget and seem uncomfortable or if you are uncertain of yourself, the interviewer will observe it. Be confident, give it your all, and most important, try to control the interview to your advantage by accentuating the benefits you have to offer.

The focus of your answers should demonstrate your ability to solve problems. Try to illustrate how you would perform on the job. Prove to the employer that he or she should hire you rather than another candidate.

Again, preparation is the key to selling yourself. You must research the company and job so that you clearly understand how your skills can solve company problems. Do research to identify the specific problems you may encounter on the job. During the interview, impress the employer with your knowledge of the company and convince him or her that you can solve the problems that the job may entail.

Show the employer that you have done your homework. Many applicants will go into the interview knowing very little about the prospective company. Speaking knowledgably about the organization and conveying enthusiasm for the job will put you ahead of most. However, be careful of overkill. Offering too much information with the intent to impress can make you come across as an obnoxious know-it-all.

Stress the employer benefits you have to offer: increasing sales, saving money, increasing proficiency, or any other benefits or accomplishments listed in Chapters 5 and 7. Illustrate your skills and abilities with stories and examples from your past work history (in particular those documented in your resume). Establish yourself as a respected and serious worker. Bring a list of references and testimonials or letters of recommendation if you have them.

Most important, display your willingness to work with others and fit into the company's image. Talk to people in the industry (employees of the firm if you can) to discover the expected image. Dress and act accordingly.

A firm handshake and direct eye contact will make an important first impression with the interviewer.

HOW TO RESEARCH A COMPANY

Talking with current employees is the best way to research a firm. Try to set up a meeting with an employee. You probably can meet some employees by checking restaurants near the company around lunchtime, or you could just call cold. Introduce yourself and explain that you have been chosen to be interviewed for a position in their company and would like some information. Learn as much as you can about the company, the job, and the interviewer (employer). Be sure to thank the employee. He or she may even put in a good word for you. The Internet has become an invaluable resource for conducting pre-interview research. Refer to Chapter 15 for more information on using the Internet for research. Also, try to find a company's mission statement. It will outline the goals of the company and will help you place your skills into their frame of reference.

Other useful resources, many of which can be accessed online, are:

- employees of competitive firms
- annual reports
- company newsletters
- local business journals
- Polk's city directories
- state directories

↱ directory of corporate affiliations
↱ *Who's Who In ...* books
↱ company employee profiles on LinkedIn

TYPES OF INTERVIEWS

In today's workforce, a variety of interview formats are widespread. Rising costs of training and keeping employees has made most companies cautious about hiring the right person. Consequently, more sophisticated interview techniques are becoming common. Familiarizing yourself with the various types of interview and question formats that you are likely to encounter in your job search is important.

SERIAL INTERVIEW

Candidates undergo a series of interviews. The initial interview is relatively simple and is intended primarily to screen out unqualified applicants. The first round of questions is geared at determining the technical qualifications and abilities of the candidate. If an applicant passes the first interview, he or she has a second, more intense interview. A variety of leading questions will be used to uncover the applicant's personality and ability to be a team player. Serial interviews are common for positions of responsibility and authority, especially managerial jobs.

SEQUENTIAL INTERVIEW

The candidate undergoes a series of interviews, but this time a different interviewer conducts each interview. The purpose is to have many interviewers judge the candidate. The decision to hire will be a group decision based upon the opinion of all those who interviewed the applicant. This method of interview is frequently used for a position that requires the employee to interact with multiple people. Each of the potential co-bosses may interview the candidate.

PANEL INTERVIEW

A panel, rather than one interviewer, questions the applicant. The panel will usually consist of people whom the candidate will be responsible to if he or she gets the job. The panel interview serves the same purpose as the sequential interview, but all interviewers are present simultaneously.

THE INSIDE SCOOP

"Our candidates go through a series of interviews. The hiring manager will ask them questions about their background and experience, and the human resource manager will ask them behavioral questions dealing with success factors and competency."

Geoff Green, VP of Talent Acquisition, Brown Shoe, Inc.

GROUP INTERVIEW

Although rarely used, in this method two or more candidates are interviewed together by one or more interviewers. This method is employed to compare the applicants face to face and often used to see which one will exert a leadership role over the others.

INTERVIEW FORMATS

STRUCTURED INTERVIEW

Each candidate is asked a series of pre-selected questions. All candidates are asked the same questions, allowing the interviewer to compare their answers easily. The upcoming sections list many frequently asked questions and explain how to answer them effectively.

UNSTRUCTURED INTERVIEW

Candidates speak freely about their past work history and accomplishments, usually from their resume. The interviewer will form an overall (subjective) picture about each candidate.

STRESS INTERVIEW

This format is also called *targeted selection interviewing*. The interviewer asks deeply probing questions to determine how well the candidate handles him or herself. Leading questions may be asked to analyze the candidate's decision-making process, and to try to make the applicant uncomfortable and unbalanced just to see the reaction. These questions are usually unexpected and the type the candidate could not have prepared for in advance, such as "What's the worst thing you've heard about our company?" "What's the worst mistake you made on your last job?" "Why did it happen?" "Whose fault was it?" (Will you blame your employer or coworkers, or will you accept the blame yourself?)

In this situation, the best strategy is *always remain calm*. Moreover, never retract what you have previously stated. Many employers want to see if you are indecisive and easily persuaded. Be calm, firm, and always exude confidence.

BEHAVIORAL INTERVIEW

Like the stress interview, the behavioral interview asks more intimidating questions that will probe your problem-solving abilities. The interviewer will ask a series of questions that require you to describe how you actually handled difficult situations. Rather than asking "What would you do if?", the interviewer will ask "What *did* you do *when*?" Recounting specific examples from the past offers the employer a good predictor for future performance.

For example, rather than ask you how you would deal with a coworker who was difficult to get along with, the employer may say, "Give me an example of a situation where you had to deal with a difficult coworker and how you handled it." Other such questions you may encounter are:

↷ Give an example of a time when you had to make a decision but did not have all the necessary information. What did you do?

↷ What was the most difficult customer-service situation you had to handle?

↷ What is the most significant contribution you made to your past employer?

↷ When was the last time you were criticized on the job? How did you respond? What did you learn from the situation?

Preparing for probing questions such as these is not easy. If asked about a situation you never experienced on the job, you may, in that case, offer a "hypothetical" answer and explain what you would do if you were to encounter such a problem. Speak with confidence and enthusiasm. Often an employer will just want to see how you react under stress. How you carry yourself can be equally or more important than the actual response. Enthusiasm, an upbeat disposition, and confidence are of utmost importance.

CASE INTERVIEW

Case interviews are especially popular in marketing and consulting firms. A case interview is one in which the candidate is presented with a case or problem similar to one you would encounter on the job and you must analyze and answer on the spot. The employer is checking your analytic reasoning skills, your ability to conceptualize, your attention to detail, your creativity, and especially your ability to communicate your ideas precisely. Often, math and other technical skills will be necessary to solve the case.

Whereas a resume and even an interview may result in the candidate offering information that is inaccurate, the case interview is always truthful. It shows the employer exactly what analytic thinking tools you are equipped with and is an indication of how you will perform on the job.

Some case interviews may involve simple brainteasers to evaluate your reasoning skills. Others can be more complicated. For example, a candidate might be asked: How many boxes of detergent were sold in St. Louis last year? Here the test is to see if you can make logical assumptions, do simple calculations, and draw logical conclusions. You might explain that there are approximately 350,000 people in St. Louis. If the average household has five members, there are 70,000 households. If each household does four loads of laundry a week and uses detergent which gives you 40 loads to a box, each family will use one box of detergent in ten weeks or approximately five to six boxes per year. If you multiply these five boxes per year times the 70,000 households, it results in approximately 350,000 boxes of detergent sold in St. Louis in one year. Usually it's not the correct answer that matters, but rather the method and thinking used to arrive at the conclusion.

Although preparing for such an interview is virtually impossible, there are some considerations to remember when being confronted with a case interview.

↷ Identify key concepts.

↷ Separate important facts from irrelevant ones.

↷ Make *reasonable* assumptions.

↷ Look for creative approaches or new insights to solving a problem.

↷ Communicate your ideas clearly and enthusiastically.

TELEPHONE INTERVIEW AND E-MAIL INTERVIEW

To reduce costs, many hiring managers are now conducting their initial screening of applicants via interviews administered by phone or e-mail. In a phone interview, the employer simply asks the applicant a list of rudimentary questions during a short phone call. The e-mail interview operates the same way. Instead of a phone call,

THE INSIDE SCOOP

"If we call a candidate at 10 o'clock in the morning and they answer in a groggy tone, it sets off a red flag. If they aren't up and about at 10, how are they going to succeed at a job that they have to get to at seven-thirty or eight in the morning? In this situation, it is better for the person not to answer at all and let the call go to voicemail. Also, they must be articulate on the phone, as well as conduct the call from a quiet room. Screaming and chaos in the background is a definite red flag."

Stephanie Yaffee and Sharon Radell
President and Agency Consultant
TLC for Kids, St. Louis, Missouri

the applicant receives an e-mail from an employer asking him to elaborate on items mentioned in his resume or to answer a list of short questions, which he then e-mails back to the employer. Both of these methods are used to evaluate candidates before inviting a selected few for a personal interview. These short interviews save the company time and money spent on unqualified applicants who can be eliminated with a simple phone call or e-mail.

For the job applicant, a marked difference exists between e-mail interviews and those conducted over the phone. In answering an e-mail, you have time to think about the questions and to formulate answers carefully before sending them back. In a phone interview, you have to answer immediately. A phone call can come at an inconvenient time, so you must always be ready. Remember that your phone interview may be recorded and played back to others involved in the hiring process.

Keeping your job search portfolio by the phone is a good strategy. Minimally, have your resume and research notes pertaining to each company easily accessible. If you have a dedicated website resume, you might suggest that the interviewer look at it while you walk him or her through it. Again, as the market becomes more competitive, these pre-interview methods are becoming more common.

COMPUTER-ASSISTED JOB INTERVIEWS

Computer-assisted job interviews are also gaining popularity due to the time and money saved by having an applicant answer multiple choice or true and false interview questions administered by a computer. This can be done at a computer station set up within the company or sometimes in one's home over the Internet. Some computer-assisted interviews are even being conducted by phone. A prerecorded message asks numerous interview questions, which the applicant answers by punching the proper digit on a touch-tone pad.

These computer interviews usually include questions about your employment history, skills, education, and even your work ethic and personal traits. Many of the tests are timed and the computer will flag questions that took you an unusually long time to answer. Studies have shown that people who are lying or trying to rationalize an inaccurate answer will spend an unusually long time answering.

A computer-assisted interview holds many advantages for the applicant, too. Most people are less self-conscious and nervous in front of the computer. The computer is not biased, so your score is the same regardless of gender or race. All applicants answer the same questions, so an employer can more easily make comparisons between them. The computer can summarize skill levels, flag inconsistencies between answers, note unusually long pauses, and sometimes suggest follow-up questions the employer can ask a candidate at a second interview conducted by a human.

Similarly, many companies are also administrating computerized personality tests and skill-level tests to assist them in evaluating the suitability of a candidate, as mentioned in Chapter 14. Today, firing an individual can result in discrimination lawsuits and other expensive legal entailments, so employers are taking every possible precaution to evaluate individuals before hiring them.

THE INTERVIEW

GETTING READY FOR THE INTERVIEW

Be sure you are clear on the date, time, and location of your interview. It cannot be stressed enough. In excitement, some people forget to make a note of the date or time and quickly forget. *Write the date, time, and place in your notebook immediately.* If possible, find out the name of the person who will be conducting the interview and write it down.

If you are unsure of the address, ask directions. Do not bother the employer, but call the company later and ask one of the secretaries or assistants for directions. Be clear on how long it will take you to arrive. Arriving late to an interview can be disastrous. If you have a GPS you can use it to check out driving directions and how long it will take to arrive. Always give yourself extra time in case you get stuck in traffic.

When you do your research before the interview, make notes on a copy of your resume. Bring that copy with you to the interview. Most interviewers will not object to your using your resume during the interview. Often during the stress of the interview, you may forget key dates or key issues you want to cover, so having your resume and notes on hand is helpful.

Be sure to bring three or four extra copies of your resume to the interview. The interviewer may need one, and may want to distribute copies to others. Additionally, bring your references (see Chapter 11), letters of recommendation, testimonials, and, if applicable, samples of your work. If you have a business card, bring some along. Furthermore, bring a pad and pen to take notes in case the interviewer gives you information to write down. Carry everything in a professional-looking briefcase or portfolio.

DRESS FOR SUCCESS

Dressing in proper attire is crucial. A candidate's overall appearance will make a lasting impression on the interviewer. Your appearance at an interview may not get you the job, but the wrong attire can lose you the job. In dressing for an interview, dress in accordance with the style of clothes worn by current employees. Accounting and finance firms may expect their personnel to wear suits in conservative colors. Advertising firms and other creative areas may be more accepting of a casual style. Learn what sort of attire is expected of you and dress accordingly. Regardless of what employees wear to work on a daily basis, you must dress nicely for an interview. If you are unsure, err on the conservative side. Additionally, looking at brochures and the website of a prospective employer will probably help you in choosing your attire.

More conservative firms usually prefer men in business suits in a neutral color such as gray, blue, or charcoal, made of a natural fiber (wool or wool blends). Wear a pressed, white shirt with a tie. A professionally laundered shirt is always best. Additionally, wear dark socks and dress shoes. Do not try to make a fashion statement; the idea is to present a professional, successful image. Most companies are very particular about the image they and their workers project, and you must fit in to work there.

Many businesses today are allowing employees to dress more casually. Casual for a man would mean a sports coat and dress slacks or khakis. However, jeans, shorts, T-shirts, caps, hiking boots, and other gym wear is frowned upon. Make no mistake: dressing inappropriately is a very easy way to make a bad impression before you even open your mouth. An employer will feel that if you do not care enough to dress in proper attire for an interview, you will not respect the company and the job.

For women, conservative clothing means something modest, such as a skirted suit made of natural fiber, cut in a classic style. A silk blouse is recommended if you can afford it. For shoes, a classic pump is best. Stay away from flashy clothes. For women, casual wear would include pantsuits, khakis, and cardigan twin sets. Wearing suggestive clothing such as low cut blouses can be a turnoff—especially if the interviewer is a woman. Many places of employment have a dress code which restricts such clothing, so wearing it to an interview is not only foolish but can cost you the job. Whatever you wear, you should remember your goal is to present a professional image. Dress in an attractive manner, but do not overdo it. If an interviewer remembers your outfit most, you may have made a fashion statement at the expense of a job.

Men and women should both be careful not to wear too much jewelry. Furthermore, do not use too much aftershave or perfume. A strong scent that is unpleasant to the interviewer or one that may cause an allergic reaction will adversely affect your chances. If you are a smoker, be sure your clothes do not smell like smoke. Tattoos and piercings can be a turn off and should not be exposed; this is especially true in a job that requires interaction with the public. Women should also be careful not to overdo their makeup. Although there is some flexibility regarding dress code, the key is to wear clothing that fits in with the job at hand and does not stand out. While someone may wear casual clothing if trying out for a job as a gym instructor, the same outfit would not be appropriate when interviewing for a position as sales manager at an upscale firm.

Come to the interview freshly bathed and groomed. Men should trim beards and mustaches, or shave. Both men and women should opt for conservative hairstyles. Use

THE INSIDE SCOOP

"Dress code is one area that has really changed over the years. I was raised to come to an interview with a navy blue suit on with brown or black shoes. Today it's totally not like that, especially in our industry, the fashion industry. Today, people can come dressed business casual. For a job at the Limited or the Gap, you might dress in the brands they sell, such as khakis. You have to fit the brand. Depending upon the industry, I rarely ever see a navy suit anymore."

—*Geoff Green, VP of Talent Acquisition, Brown Shoe, Inc.*

deodorant, brush your teeth, and be sure your nails are clean. The interviewer will consciously and subconsciously take *everything* into account. Present a conservative and professional image and you will be fine.

ARRIVING AT THE INTERVIEW

Arrive five or ten minutes early if possible. However, do not arrive earlier than that. Employers tend to get nervous when an applicant is sitting around waiting to be interviewed. Before leaving your house, make sure you have the employer's phone number with you. If an unsuspected emergency occurs and you will be late, you can call and tell them. He or she may want to reschedule your interview.

Come in rested and mentally prepared. Spend time reviewing your resume and readying yourself for the interview. Wait until the interviewer introduces himself or herself and offers his or her hand, before offering yours. Never use the interviewer's first name unless told to do so, and wait for instructions before taking a seat.

THE QUESTIONS

WHAT TO EXPECT

Questions will cover the following areas:

- education
- work experience
- career goals
- personality and motivation
- reasons for changing jobs
- stress questions
- salary and benefits

The employer has specific worries about hiring you and will use the interview to dispel these fears. The major ones include:

- Do you require constant supervision?
- Are you only interested in the paycheck?
- How well will you get along with coworkers?
- Will your social life affect your job?
- Do you use your time productively?
- Will you be loyal to the company?
- Are you honest and reliable?
- Will you be content with the salary and working conditions?

Once you recognize the motivation behind the questions, your answers can help dispel the employer's fears. Always present yourself as a problem solver, energetic, willing to work hard, and someone who fits in with the company culture. If you make it clear that you love your work and are willing to work hard, you will be a top candidate for the job.

TIPS ON ANSWERING QUESTIONS

First and foremost, *never lie*. According to the Burke, Inc. marketing survey, lying and dishonesty rank as the number one trait employers find objectionable. Even if you were fired from a previous job, do not conceal it. If asked for details, explain what happened but qualify it. Tell the employer what you learned from the experience and why it will never happen again. Remember, most employers will check candidates before hiring them, so do not lie to make yourself look better—it could cost you the job.

Always make eye contact. Answer with confidence and try not to get flustered. If the employer tries to throw you off, remember it is an interview tactic to see how well you handle stress and how fast you are on your feet. Employers harshly judge people who cannot make up their minds or take a stand. Many equate uncertainty with instability or incompetence, traits employers find undesirable. Never lose your cool. Think before talking, and answer with confidence and authority.

People hire people they like. Show some interest in the interviewer and the company. Always be courteous. Learn the interviewers name and use it (but not until you're instructed to do so).

Finally, do not cover up your nervousness by talking too much. Listen when the interviewer speaks. Do not interrupt. If you have a question, wait until the interviewer has finished talking.

ILLEGAL QUESTIONS

Sometimes an interviewer will ask an illegal question such as "Are you married?" Sometimes an interviewer is just making small talk to relax you. Occasionally, it is an illegal screening device.

Usually not making an issue of the matter is the best strategy. If you become angry, you will probably not get the job. If you feel you have been discriminated against, you can bring a lawsuit. Be forewarned: you will have a difficult time proving you did not get the job due to discrimination. Worse yet, if you get a reputation as being difficult you may find it impossible to get any job.

The best thing to do is to dispel the employer's worry, and answer, "Yes, I am married, but my family totally supports my career decisions and I never let my family life affect my job performance." If the question is one that truly upsets your sensibilities, you may simply ask the interviewer to explain how the information he or she requests is relevant to the job at hand. This will usually stop the interviewer from proceeding with similar questions.

AFTER THE INTERVIEW

QUESTIONS *You* SHOULD ASK

At the end of the interview, you may be asked if you have any questions. Even if you are not asked directly, you should interject, "Do you mind if I ask a few questions?" Asking questions shows that you are genuinely interested in the position.

However, you will be judged by your questions. Therefore, do not ask about salary and promotions. The interviewer may get a negative message that you are interested mainly in the paycheck. Additionally, do not ask what the organization or department does. A question like this shows you didn't care enough about the position to learn beforehand.

Ask questions about *the job*. This will display your interest and will supply you with the information you will need to decide if the job is right for you.

Questions you may want to ask include:

↪ To whom will I report?

↪ How do you see your company developing over the next few years?

- Is this a new position or will I be replacing someone?
- What happened to the last person who held this position?
- How many people have held this position in the last five years?
- What would be your highest priority for me to accomplish if you hired me?

LEAVING THE INTERVIEW

The interview is not over until you have left the premises. Offer a firm handshake and leave on a positive note. Express your thankfulness to the interviewer, complimenting him or her, and mentioning that you are eagerly looking forward to hearing from him or her.

One more note: always be courteous to the secretaries and assistants. Extend courtesies to the secretaries upon both entering and leaving the interview. Often they will be asked for their opinion about a candidate, so show respect to everyone you meet.

TAKING NOTES—A RETROSPECTIVE

Immediately upon leaving the interview, take out your workbook. Be sure you have the correct spelling of the interviewer's name. Make notes on how you feel the interview went. What do you think could have made it better? Note any questions that stumped you. This is a great way to prepare for both the second stage and your next interview.

CHECKING YOUR REFERENCES

If the interviewer is interested in hiring you, he or she will check your references. Understand that your former boss will be asked questions such as the following:

- How long has the applicant worked for you?
- How was the quality of the applicant's work?
- How did the applicant get along with you? With fellow workers?
- How much supervision did the applicant require?
- Who else could I talk to about the applicant?

THE FOLLOW-UP

Immediately upon returning home from the interview, write a follow-up thank-you letter. Look at the sample letters in Chapter 13.

THE INSIDE SCOOP

"Thank you notes are still customary. However, nowadays, it's not necessarily the written note but an e-mail is fine. It's good if the applicant not only conveys their appreciation for the interview but it's also important to me if they put something in the letter that they remember from the interview that demonstrates they were listening, too. Some type of follow up is always important. Even a phone call is ok, although I personally prefer an e-mail."

—*Geoff Green, VP of Talent Acquisition, Brown Shoe, Inc.*

The letter should include two components. The first paragraph should be a courteous thank you for the interview. The second paragraph should reiterate why you want the job and what you can do for the company. It can be a recap of something you stressed during the interview or a new angle you thought of after the interview. Close with a statement that expresses your enthusiasm.

Wait one week and follow up with a phone call. If you do not get the job, ask the employer candidly for some constructive criticism on your interview technique. Note it in your job journal. This can greatly assist you in preparing for future interviews.

THE MOCK INTERVIEW

The best way to prepare for an interview is to conduct a mock interview. Have a friend play the role of the employer and ask you the following questions. Record your answers on audio or, better yet, video. Do not study the suggested answers yet. Listen to the playback. Compare your answers with the suggested answers. How do your answers compare?

Grade yourself on such qualities as your ability to communicate, confidence, enthusiasm, energy level, and intelligence. On video you can also judge such things as whether you maintained eye contact, smiled during the interview, fidgeted, sat straight, were attentive to the interviewer, and came across as someone you would like and could trust.

FREQUENTLY ASKED INTERVIEW QUESTIONS

DESCRIBE A TYPICAL WORKING DAY

Do your research and know the skills that are required in the job for which you are interviewing. Construct your answer to emphasize those skills in describing your typical day. Paint a picture of yourself as a hard worker, a problem solver, and an enthusiastic person.

For example, if the job you are seeking requires accuracy in report writing, you might say: "I spend much of my day writing reports. I put in significant effort checking and double checking. I always want to be positive that everything is accurate."

WHY ARE YOU INTERESTED IN WORKING FOR US?

Stress the company's excellent reputation and the exciting direction it is taking. Here your research will come in handy. Cite impressive things you have heard or read about the company. You may emphasize how well you feel you will fit in with the company's image and expectations. Being familiar with the company's mission statement before the interview and mentioning how your viewpoint and sensibilities match theirs can also make a good impression. Not only does it show that you have done your homework and are familiar with the company but it also demonstrates that you share the same perspective they do.

If the company is small and does not have an outstanding reputation, you will want to stress that you enjoy working for small companies where you can distinguish yourself. If you have done your research and understand how your skills can benefit this particular company's needs, suggest that in your answer too.

WHAT IS YOUR MAJOR WEAKNESS?

Do not be foolish enough to say you do not have any. Everyone has weaknesses. The idea is to mention one weak spot you are working at strengthening. "I used to take on too many projects at once. Recently I attended a seminar on time management and I've found myself being more productive than ever." You may also talk about a skill area you are working on improving. You may add, "My computer skills were not where I would like them to be so I am presently taking additional computer training in my spare time." Showing that you are someone who takes the initiative to improve yourself will certainly make a favorable impression on a future boss.

TELL ME ABOUT YOURSELF. WHAT ARE YOUR GREATEST STRENGTHS?

This is not a biographical question. Your answer should stress your skills and abilities. "I'm a hard worker," "I'm a person with a good eye for detail," "I enjoy a job that lets me use my talents," are good answers. You may want to emphasize some of the major projects you worked on and the successes you have had. You may choose to talk about how you put yourself through school by working. Regardless, everything you tell about yourself should pertain to the job at hand and project a professional image. Most people like to hear stories more than hard facts. Tell about situations that illustrate problems you solved, rather than just talking in the abstract about your skills and abilities. Just like you did in your resume, emphasize the "employer benefits" that you brought to your previous job and/or the benefits you can bring to this job as well. Remember employer benefits are the reason an employer will hire you and to the employer, these benefits are more important than pure skill and ability.

WHAT DO YOU THINK OF YOUR PREVIOUS BOSS?

Never be critical. Never complain. Above all, do not vilify any previous boss. Doing so will tag you as trouble. Be positive and say something such as "I respect my former boss and learned a lot from him. I am seeking other employment because the opportunities for growth at my former company are limited."

WHERE DO YOU SEE YOURSELF FIVE YEARS FROM NOW?

The employer wants to be certain your plans do not include leaving the company after being trained. Emphasize your desire to be part of a winning team and to remain with them. You may say, "I plan to be here, advancing my career, and making satisfying accomplishments."

TELL ME ABOUT YOUR EDUCATION. WHAT SUBJECTS DID YOU EXCEL IN?

Stress those subjects and areas of study that directly pertain to the job at hand. Mention stories and projects that demonstrate you have drive, possess motivation, and take initiative to do jobs properly.

GIVE A DEFINITION OF A ... (JOB TITLE YOU ARE INTERVIEWING FOR).

The definition should be task oriented, defined by the responsibilities and accomplishments expected. For example, a data processor is someone responsible for accurately entering data so that meaningful reports and money-saving decisions will be produced.

WHAT DO YOU LIKE TO DO IN YOUR SPARE TIME?

Mention activities that supplement and enhance your career goals. Examples are attending workshops, reading trade magazines, and attending conventions. You may want to include activities that show you care about your health and well-being, such as exercise and fitness classes. Steer away from anything political or controversial.

WHAT WAS THE LAST GOOD BOOK YOU READ OR YOUR MOST FAVORITE RECENT MOVIE?

This has become a popular question in today's market. Even social media sites such as LinkedIn are featuring members' "reading lists." If you are not certain what type of book the employer feels is important for his employees to read, you may answer that you have been so busy with your job search that you haven't had time to read for pleasure. If you have read a book that pertains to your occupation, mentioning it would most likely make a good impression on the employer. Don't mention a book you haven't actually read; the employer may have read it and ask you questions about it.

WHY WERE YOU FIRED FROM YOUR LAST JOB?

Do not lie. Many people will tell the interviewer that they were released due to cutbacks. Remember, this information can be easily verified in a short phone call to your last employer. Do not talk negatively about your former employer or coworkers, as this sort of negativism will ruin your chance of getting the job.

Explain what happened and take responsibility for your mistakes. However, be sure to tell the interviewer what you learned and gained from the experience and why you are now a better employee.

You may also qualify your termination by stating something like, "They needed someone who was more skilled in the area of ___" or "My interests and strengths lie more in the area of ___." (Mention a strength that is crucial in the job for which you are interviewing.)

WHAT DO YOU KNOW ABOUT OUR COMPANY?

If you have done your research, this is where you can shine. Knowing the company's mission statement is a plus as well. If you have not been able to find out very much about the company, minimally try to impress upon the interviewer that you made an earnest albeit unsuccessful, attempt to gather information.

If the company has been in business for many years, you can honestly say, "Because I plan to stick with one company for a long time, I seek out stable companies with a strong reputation, such as yours."

WHAT CAN YOU DO FOR US THAT OTHER CANDIDATES CANNOT?

Stress the benefits you can offer to the employer, your qualifications, and your ability to save the employer money. Be sure to stress some of your marketable personality traits, such as being a team player, a quick learner, and having strong communication skills. Stress your loyalty, dedication, and desire to remain with one company for the duration of your career.

HOW WOULD YOU DESCRIBE YOUR PERSONALITY?

Again, stress the positive. Describe the self-management skills you possess that would be most desired for your job, such as an ability to be a team player, an eye for accuracy, an ability to maximize time, and your honesty and integrity.

WHAT INTERESTS YOU MOST ABOUT THIS JOB?

If you are aware of specific problems that you will be required to solve, mention those and explain that the *challenge* of solving these problems and the *opportunity to contribute* to the company excites you. If this job offers *more responsibility,* you could mention that, too.

DO YOU WORK BETTER ALONE OR IN A GROUP?

Again, researching and understanding the nature of the job at hand is crucial. If the job for which you are interviewing requires working in a team, then obviously the answer to this question is working in a group. The employer is looking for you to assure him or her that you are a team player.

WHY HAVE YOU CHANGED JOBS SO FREQUENTLY?

You can stress that your job changes were a result of your desire to gain diverse experience and develop a multitude of skills. Holding different positions was a growing experience that has given you a broader awareness of the workforce than most candidates. Be careful not to mention money as the prime motivating factor in changing jobs.

Another approach is to explain that you needed to try different careers before you could settle down with the one best suited for you. Tell the employer you are now confident you have made the choice for your future and are ready to settle down with one company and one job.

HOW MUCH MONEY DO YOU WANT TO MAKE?

Never give a specific figure. You may price yourself out of the job or, worse yet, you may undersell yourself. Be vague. Answer with a general range, such as "Between $25,000 and $30,000 dollars."

Alternatively, you could ask outright, "What does the job pay?" After hearing the employer's answer, you can add that the pay is within the range or ballpark figure you had in mind.

ADDITIONAL QUESTIONS FOR RECENT GRADUATES

- ↪ Why did you attend ___ (your college or career school)?
- ↪ Why did you major in ___?
- ↪ What was your grade point average?
- ↪ Why were your grades so low? Did you do your best?
- ↪ What would you change about your education if you could?
- ↪ How did you finance your education?
- ↪ Tell me about some of your accomplishments.
- ↪ What extracurricular activities did you participate in?

  Use the following worksheets to prepare for your interviews.

SEARCH AND RESEARCH

Although the above list is fairly comprehensive, it is not complete by any means. You can find even more interview questions if you do an Internet search on "mock interview questions," or just plain "interview questions." You will discover many websites that supply lists of interview questions for you to think about. Even more useful resources for mock interviews can be found on YouTube. Doing a search for "interview questions" will unearth many interesting mock interview videos that may prove very helpful. You may also consider querying your LinkedIn contacts for any suggestions they may have regarding interview questions and answers specific to your occupation.

CHAPTER 18 / WORKSHEET

THE JOB INTERVIEW

PREPARING FOR THE INTERVIEW

COMPANY NAME: _____

POSITION: _____

DATE OF INTERVIEW: _____

TIME OF INTERVIEW: _____

PHONE NUMBER: _____

EMPLOYER'S (INTERVIEWER'S) NAME: _____

ADDRESS: _____

_____

TRAVELING INSTRUCTIONS: _____

_____

_____

TRAVEL TIME: _____

COMPANY DESCRIPTION (Background—Products—Services): _____

_____

_____

_____

_____

COMPANY'S MAIN COMPETITORS: _____

MISSION STATEMENT: _____

_____

_____

SKILLS REQUIRED FOR THE JOB (compare want ad): _____

_____

_____

_____

CONTRIBUTIONS I CAN MAKE: _____

_____

_____

_____

SALARY RANGE: _____

(continued)

CHAPTER 18 WORKSHEET (CONTINUED)

THE JOB INTERVIEW

INTERVIEW CHECKLIST

☐ Resume—3 copies   ☐ Business cards

☐ References   ☐ Samples of work

☐ Letters of recommendation   ☐ Writing pad and pen

☐ Professional briefcase or portfolio (to hold everything)

AFTER THE INTERVIEW

QUESTIONS THAT WERE DIFFICULT: _____

_____

_____

_____

_____

_____

_____

_____

_____

INTROSPECTION (How I did or how I could improve my interview):

_____

_____

_____

_____

_____

_____

_____

_____

_____

FOLLOW-UP CHECKLIST

☐ Thank-you letter   ☐ Second interview

☐ Phone call

FINAL OUTCOME

_____

_____

_____

CHAPTER 18 / WORKSHEET

THE JOB INTERVIEW

PREPARING FOR THE INTERVIEW

COMPANY NAME: _____

POSITION: _____

DATE OF INTERVIEW: _____

TIME OF INTERVIEW: _____

PHONE NUMBER: _____

EMPLOYER'S (INTERVIEWER'S) NAME: _____

ADDRESS: _____

_____

TRAVELING INSTRUCTIONS: _____

_____

_____

TRAVEL TIME: _____

COMPANY DESCRIPTION (Background—Products—Services): _____

_____

_____

_____

_____

COMPETITORS: _____

SKILLS REQUIRED FOR THE JOB (compare want ad): _____

_____

_____

_____

CONTRIBUTIONS I CAN MAKE: _____

_____

_____

_____

SALARY RANGE: _____

(continued)

CHAPTER 18 / WORKSHEET (CONTINUED)

THE JOB INTERVIEW

INTERVIEW CHECKLIST

☐ Resume—3 copies

☐ References

☐ Letters of recommendation

☐ Professional briefcase or portfolio (to hold everything)

☐ Business cards

☐ Samples of work

☐ Writing pad and pen

AFTER THE INTERVIEW

QUESTIONS THAT WERE DIFFICULT: _____

_____

_____

_____

_____

_____

_____

_____

_____

INTROSPECTION (How I did or how I could improve my interview):

_____

_____

_____

_____

_____

_____

_____

_____

_____

FOLLOW-UP CHECKLIST

☐ Thank-you letter

☐ Phone call

☐ Second interview

FINAL OUTCOME

_____

_____

_____

CHAPTER 18 WORKSHEET

THE JOB INTERVIEW

PREPARING FOR THE INTERVIEW

COMPANY NAME: _____

POSITION: _____

DATE OF INTERVIEW: _____

TIME OF INTERVIEW: _____

PHONE NUMBER: _____

EMPLOYER'S (INTERVIEWER'S) NAME: _____

ADDRESS: _____

_____

TRAVELING INSTRUCTIONS: _____

_____

_____

TRAVEL TIME: _____

COMPANY DESCRIPTION (Background—Products—Services): _____

_____

_____

_____

_____

COMPETITORS: _____

SKILLS REQUIRED FOR THE JOB (compare want ad): _____

_____

_____

_____

CONTRIBUTIONS I CAN MAKE: _____

_____

_____

_____

SALARY RANGE: _____

(continued)

CHAPTER 18 WORKSHEET (CONTINUED)

THE JOB INTERVIEW

INTERVIEW CHECKLIST

☐ Resume—3 copies

☐ References

☐ Letters of recommendation

☐ Professional briefcase or portfolio (to hold everything)

☐ Business cards

☐ Samples of work

☐ Writing pad and pen

AFTER THE INTERVIEW

QUESTIONS THAT WERE DIFFICULT: _____

_____

_____

_____

_____

_____

_____

_____

_____

INTROSPECTION (How I did or how I could improve my interview):

_____

_____

_____

_____

_____

_____

_____

_____

_____

_____

FOLLOW-UP CHECKLIST

☐ Thank-you letter

☐ Phone call

☐ Second interview

FINAL OUTCOME

_____

_____

_____

CHAPTER 19

PERSONAL JOB JOURNAL

☑ Excellent
☐ Very good
☐ Good
☐ Average

Prepare to Succeed ⟫⟫

In this final chapter you will find journal pages designed to help you keep track of your job search progress. There are journal entries for the contacts you've already made and for potential contacts you will want to call. There is both a weekly and monthly calendar to enter dates for appointments and to schedule timely follow up phone calls and correspondence. With a calendar built in to virtually every e-mail service, you can transfer your schedule online, enabling you to access it from any computer anywhere. New to this edition is a journal entry for potential Facebook or LinkedIn contacts. Keeping a journal is imperative. It keeps you organized and helps you stay focused, and staying focused will ultimately get you a job.

THREE PURPOSES OF THE JOURNAL

This personal job journal is designed to meet four goals:

↪ to help you generate a list of potential employers;

↪ to track your progress with your target market;

↪ to notify and remind you when you need to place follow-up calls and/or send follow-up documents; and

↪ to keep a record of which version of your resume and which correspondence was sent to whom.

GENERATING A TARGET MARKET LIST

To create a constructive list of employers (those looking to hire someone with your credentials), you will have to endure some preliminary steps. Secondary contacts will lead you to primary contacts, which will after some effort result in a master list: your target market.

SECONDARY CONTACTS/RESEARCH

Record the names of friends and acquaintances who can assist you. Ask them to supply you with the names of people in your field that they personally know. If they do not know anyone, try to at least get the names of other people they know who might help you.

Use your library's resources to uncover potential contacts in your field.

Use your library's resources to get the names of employees at all local businesses in your field. Try to determine which person at each firm is in charge of hiring. Record these leads as primary contacts.

PRIMARY CONTACTS

Any business or organization that employs people in your field is a primary contact. Call all of these businesses. Find out if they are hiring and how the process works at their company. Try to reach the person in charge of hiring—even if no job is presently available. Introduce yourself to that person. If you were referred to him or her by one of your secondary contacts, mention that person's name.

Even if no job is available, ask if you can send a copy of your resume for future reference. Better yet, set up an informational interview. Move any primary contact that expresses an interest in you to your master list—target market.

If a primary contact shows no interest, ask if they know someone else who is looking to hire. If they do, write that person's name on your list of primary contacts. Contact that person next, mentioning the name of the person who just referred you to him or her. Names carry weight, so use them whenever possible.

WEB CONTACTS

You will want to keep track of everyone you have contacted on the web. For contacts on Facebook or LinkedIn, just check in to see if they have contacted you, or if they have posted information in their profile or pages. However, you will want to keep a paper record of all the e-mail addresses and the URLs of the company and job boards that you frequent. The Internet can be a maze, and it's all too easy to forget which sites were helpful. *Document everything.*

Pay particular attention to those websites where you posted your resume. Record the date you posted your resume and how long it will stay on that particular job board. Tag or number (code) each version of your resume, and include each one in your job search portfolio. Make a note of which version you posted on which sites. You can enter the version code on your contact sheet also, and thus easily track which version of your resume you sent to whom.

Similarly, track which online ads you answered. Print out the ads for your job search portfolio and code them. On your job journal contact sheet, enter the code under the heading "Job Description and Number," making it easy to track which job postings you answered.

MASTER LIST—TARGET MARKET

From your list of primary contacts (those you have phoned) select those who indicated an interest in you and record them on your master list. Concentrate on these contacts. They are the employers who are most likely to hire you.

Strategize. Write what you can do for each company in a tailored cover letter. Be sure each of the contacts on your master list gets a copy of your resume with a personalized cover letter. Better yet, set up a meeting with the person in charge of hiring. Do not be a nuisance, but follow up often enough that he or she will remember you. Anytime a primary contact expresses interest in you, he or she becomes a member of your target market, and you should record him or her on your master list.

WANT ADS ANSWERED

Although you should not place too much faith in want ads, answering a legitimate ad never hurts. Keep track of the ads you have answered and the date. Follow up if possible, and record all results. Add any employer that shows an interest in you to your master list, even if he or she does not hire you. Follow up later.

WEEKLY/MONTHLY PLANNER

Be organized. Set aside time daily to make calls and send out resumes and cover letters. Record all your activities: meetings, phone calls, and resumes sent. Additionally, record all your tasks, such as follow-up letters and phone calls that you must make at later dates, as well as any scheduled interviews. Most importantly, check your calendar every morning.

KEEP FINDING CONTACTS AND KEEP MAKING CALLS. BE PERSISTENT AND YOU WILL GET A JOB SOONER THAN YOU THINK!

SECONDARY CONTACTS

Think of at least 15 people—friends, relatives, business associates, organization members—who can supply you with leads (names of potential employers). Write their names below and get their phone numbers. Call them. On your list of Primary Contacts record the names of potential employers they give you.

	Name	Phone Number	✓ Done
1.			
2.			
3.			
4.			
5.			
6.			
7.			
8.			
9.			
10.			
11.			
12.			
13.			
14.			
15.			
16.			
17.			
18.			
19.			
20.			

SOCIAL MEDIA SOURCES

These are contacts you may have come across on your Facebook or LinkedIn account that you will want to contact. You should also enter how you will make contact with them—either directly by e-mail, phone, social media, or through a mutual contact.

	Sources to contact	How to make contact
1.		
2.		
3.		
4.		
5.		
6.		
7.		
8.		
9.		
10.		

RESEARCH SOURCES

Write down the titles of resource materials (websites, directories, trade journals, and periodicals) that you will check for leads. Check these sources for the names of companies and/or people hiring. Again, enter all *potential* employers on your list of Primary Contacts. Next, check out these new contacts on LinkedIn to see if they are members of a network or group. Better yet, check if anyone in your network is connected to any of these potential contacts and see if they are willing to make a connection for you.

	Sources	✓ Done
1.		
2.		
3.		
4.		
5.		
6.		
7.		
8.		
9.		
10.		
11.		
12.		
13.		
14.		
15.		
16.		
17.		
18.		
19.		
20.		
21.		
22.		
23.		
24.		
25.		

WANT ADS ANSWERED

Name of the Firm	Address or Blind Box #	Name and Date of Publication of Opening	Date Answered	Results

PRIMARY CONTACTS

Name of the Firm	Phone Number	Contact's Name and Title	Referred to By (Person/Source)	Results

CONTACTS MADE ONLINE

Name	Address	Phone	E-mail Address	Web Site

RESUMES POSTED ONLINE

Board	URL	Post Date	Expiration Date	Resume Version

JOB POSTS ANSWERED ONLINE

Board	Date	Job Description and Number	Destination URL

CORRESPONDENCE SENT OUT

Every version of your resume should be identified with a unique number, such as resume1.doc or resume_teacher.doc. Each version should be kept in a notebook or in a computer file for easy retrieval. Every major version of your cover letter should also be filed and identified. The same should hold true for all major correspondence, such as follow-up thank-you letters. You should then keep a journal entry to indicate which resume, cover letter, and follow-up correspondence went out to whom.

Resume version	Cover letter	Other Correspondence	Sent to:	Date

MASTER LIST—TARGET MARKET

Call Number	Contact's Name & Title	Phone Number	Firm's Name and Address	Dates of Action					Results
				Resume	Meeting	Letter	FollowUp	FollowUp	

WEEKLY PLANNER

MONTH: _____ WEEK# _____

To Do:		Phone Calls / Meetings / etc.	✓ Done
Mon:	8:00		
	9:00		
	10:00		
	11:00		
	12:00		
	1:00		
	2:00		
	3:00		
	4:00		
	5:00		
Tues:	8:00		
	9:00		
	10:00		
	11:00		
	12:00		
	1:00		
	2:00		
	3:00		
	4:00		
	5:00		
Wed:	8:00		
	9:00		
	10:00		
	11:00		
	12:00		
	1:00		
	2:00		
	3:00		
	4:00		
	5:00		
Thur:	8:00		
	9:00		
	10:00		
	11:00		
	12:00		
	1:00		
	2:00		
	3:00		
	4:00		
	5:00		
Fri:	8:00		
	9:00		
	10:00		
	11:00		
	12:00		
	1:00		
	2:00		
	3:00		
	4:00		
	5:00		

MONTHLY PLANNER

Sunday	Monday	Tuesday	Wednesday	Thursday	Friday	Saturday

P = Phone Call   R = Resume   L = Letter   I = Interview

SECONDARY CONTACTS

Think of at least 15 people—friends, relatives, business associates, organization members, anyone—who can supply you with leads (names of potential employers). Write their names below and get their phone numbers. Call them. Record on your list of Primary Contacts the names of potential employers they give you.

	Name	Phone Number	✓ Done
1.			
2.			
3.			
4.			
5.			
6.			
7.			
8.			
9.			
10.			
11.			
12.			
13.			
14.			
15.			
16.			
17.			
18.			
19.			
20.			
21.			
22.			
23.			
24.			
25.			

RESEARCH SOURCES

Write down the titles of resource materials (websites, directories, trade journals, and periodicals) that you will check for leads. Ask your librarian for assistance. Check these sources for the names of companies and/or people hiring. Again, enter all *potential* employers on your list of Primary Contacts. Next, check out these new contacts on LinkedIn to see if they are members of a network or group. Better yet, check if anyone in your network is connected to any of these potential contacts and see if they are willing to make a connection for you.

	Sources	✓ Done
1.		
2.		
3.		
4.		
5.		
6.		
7.		
8.		
9.		
10.		
11.		
12.		
13.		
14.		
15.		
16.		
17.		
18.		
19.		
20.		
21.		
22.		
23.		
24.		
25.		

WANT ADS ANSWERED

Name of the Firm	Address or Blind Box #	Name and Date of Publication of Opening	Date Answered	Results

PRIMARY CONTACTS

Name of the Firm	Phone Number	Contact's Name and Title	Referred to By (Person/Source)	Results

CONTACTS MADE ONLINE

Name	Address	Phone	E-mail Address	Web Site

RESUMES POSTED ONLINE

Board	URL	Post Date	Expiration Date	Resume Version

JOB POSTS ANSWERED ONLINE

Board	Date	Job Description and Number	Destination URL

CORRESPONDENCE SENT OUT

Every version of your resume should be identified with a unique number, such as resume1.doc or resume_teacher.doc. Each version should be kept in a notebook or in a computer file for easy retrieval. Every major version of your cover letter should also be filed and identified. The same should hold true for all major correspondence, such as follow-up thank-you letters. You should then keep a journal entry to indicate which resume, cover letter, and follow-up correspondence went out to whom.

Resume version	Cover letter	Other Correspondence	Sent to:	Date

MASTER LIST—TARGET MARKET

Call Number	Contact's Name & Title	Phone Number	Firm's Name and Address	Dates of Action					Results
				Resume	Meeting	Letter	FollowUp	FollowUp	

WEEKLY PLANNER

MONTH: _____ WEEK# _____

To Do:		Phone Calls / Meetings / etc.	✓ Done
Mon:	8:00		
	9:00		
	10:00		
	11:00		
	12:00		
	1:00		
	2:00		
	3:00		
	4:00		
	5:00		
Tues:	8:00		
	9:00		
	10:00		
	11:00		
	12:00		
	1:00		
	2:00		
	3:00		
	4:00		
	5:00		
Wed:	8:00		
	9:00		
	10:00		
	11:00		
	12:00		
	1:00		
	2:00		
	3:00		
	4:00		
	5:00		
Thur:	8:00		
	9:00		
	10:00		
	11:00		
	12:00		
	1:00		
	2:00		
	3:00		
	4:00		
	5:00		
Fri:	8:00		
	9:00		
	10:00		
	11:00		
	12:00		
	1:00		
	2:00		
	3:00		
	4:00		
	5:00		

MONTHLY PLANNER

Sunday	Monday	Tuesday	Wednesday	Thursday	Friday	Saturday

P = Phone Call   R = Resume   L = Letter   I = Interview

INDEX